NICHE MARKETING

for Writers, Speakers, and Entrepreneurs

How to Make Yourself Indispensable, Slightly Immortal, and Lifelong Rich in 18 Months!

WARNING — DISCLAIMER

NICHE MARKETING

for Writers, Speakers, and Entrepreneurs

How to Make Yourself Indispensable,
Slightly Immortal, and
Lifelong Rich in 18 Months!

GORDON BURGETT

COMMUNICATION UNLIMITED
Santa Maria, California

ABOUT THE AUTHOR

Gordon Burgett has been writing and speaking about the processes of writing, speaking, and related entrepreneurship for more than 30 years. With over 1,500 items in print, an annual speaking schedule of 100 presentations and seminars, some 16 tape singles and series in existence, and a series of information dissemination-related reports currently published, he has also been a publisher since 1981. In earlier incarnations Burgett earned four academic degrees, played professional baseball, participated in a gold hunt up the Napo and Paushi-Yaco Rivers, and directed a CARE program in Colombia and Ecuador. His most recent books, of ten, are *Self-Publishing to Tightly-Targeted Markets, The Travel Writer's Guide, The Writer's Guide to Query Letters and Cover Letters, How to Sell More Than 75% of Your Freelance Writing, Empire-Building by Writing and Speaking, Speaking for Money (with Mike Frank),* and *Ten Sales From One Article Idea.* Six times Burgett's books have been Writer's Digest Book Club selections. He currently lives in Santa Maria, California.

ISBN 0-910167-22-2

Published by Communication Unlimited, P.O. Box 6405,
Santa Maria, California 93456
(805) 937-8711/FAX (805) 937-3035

Table of Contents

Special appreciation to Patricia Manuras, my favorite proofreader, a clever and humorous soul who again lost the fight to save you, the readers, from my occasional deviations into mirth.

To Dan Poynter and Tyler Kieswetter for valuable advise and information about, respectively, publishing/speaking and mass mailing.

And to Judy Capitana, who graphically prepared the cover and kindly encouraged me not to fill all of the white space with useless copy, come-ons, and other comehitherish extras.

For anything else I also take the blame.

Introduction

My claim that you can make yourself indispensable, slightly immortal, and lifelong rich in 18 months *does* sound preposterous — like a crafty con to wheedle you out of $14.95, plus tax (and probably shipping).

Yet if you don't read what the book says, I can almost guarantee you that it won't happen for you this way. Any more than it did in the past 18 months.

Niche Marketing for Writers, Speakers, and Entrepreneurs takes you on a truly gilded path now open to information disseminators and the entrepreneurs who hover about them. By the last page you will see that the claim is indeed modest rather than fanciful or in any way deceptive.

The pages that follow explain a thought process, what you must do to make it succeed, and the key means by which those achievements and rewards can be yours.

Alas, I can't give you courage. Nor can I make you work. For success here both are required.

Nor does it hurt to be a bit hungry. Not in the empty-stomach sense, but champing to get ahead, to improve your lot, quickly and by much.

Some seed money will also accelerate the process. Several thousand dollars are probably enough, to get going and later to hire others to do those rare things that you do poorly or indifferently. But even there, if your pockets are light, you can probably earn a sufficient starting ante from clever thinking and extra application, and from those first profits finance your future growth.

Niche marketing is the new frontier of the information revolution. This book is a map to that frontier. Savor the joy of adventure into this new, needed land where you prosper by sharing valuable information with others. What could be more exciting?

Why, then, are we dawdling? The premise follows!

Chapter 1

The Premise

Can every reader of these pages make themselves indispensable, slightly immortal, and lifelong rich in 18 months? Probably not. Yet in that year and a half they could be properly planted on the path to wealth and well on their way to achieving all three goals.

How long, then, might it take *you* to reach six-figuredom? Quickly. Seven figures might take a few more months, a year, two, five — maybe never. The timing is really up to you and how well you apply the broad suggestions on these pages — how much you do, how you do it, and when.

What specifically *must* you do to achieve those goals?
Sell information.
How vital or crucial the information is to the buyer, how unique or singularly shared, and how clearly and well you can impart it will determine your indispensability.
How profoundly it is offered will govern the depth and degree of your immortality.
And how you sell it, how much you sell, and what you charge will directly affect your income and profits.
The eighteen months is a guesstimate on my part. It's too long for some: they'll be in fatcat city in half that time, or sooner. It's too short for others, who will nibble at the process, dabble at it while trying a dozen other strategies, tiptoe stealthily into new areas, timidly probe at the new means. Some will never receive the benefits. They are terrified of success or flat-out refuse to see

the obvious, and simply won't work with sufficient vigor and finesse to make their dreams come true. And some just bought this book to carry around. (It doesn't work vicariously or osmotically.)

Later we will discuss the kind of information that is salable and how you sell it, plus all of the steps needed to reach the three goals.

Now, let me offer a rough, opening example of how one might realize these goals by taking a crucial piece of knowledge through the major steps of its developmental and marketing life.

Let's say you are an insurance agent who primarily sells policies to dentists.

You could continue selling insurance and earn a fairly reliable $45,000 a year. Or you could retire in about three years with well over a million dollars in the bank. The difference is what you do with a particular piece of information: you know that dentists pay thousands of dollars a year for malpractice insurance — and you know how dentists can cut those malpractice premiums in half.

There are 125,000 practicing dentists in the U.S. If you wrote a book called *Dentists: How to Lower Your Malpractice Insurance Premiums 50%*, priced it at $19.95, offered it by mail to every dentist, and sold it to 10% of the total, that alone would bring you approximately $180,000 in profit — 50% of it within four weeks of the mailing of the sales flyers, 98% within 13 weeks. (We'll review the expense/income breakdown in Chapter 13.)

A NEWSLETTER

Yet a book is a static exchange: its contents are frozen on the page. And insurance premiums, the range and kind of coverage, and industry policies are dynamic, as are the laws and practices concerning malpractice. So to keep your clients currently appraised you decide to offer a quarterly newsletter. It will update the contents of the book every three months plus provide significantly more information about insurance and dentistry written in lay language. The newsletter would be an excellent guide, really the final word, to that particular facet of dental business: full of facts, objective, directed specifically to dentists and their staff, even fun to read.

How would they know about it? Three ways. It would be advertised on a double page at the end of your book. You will send a follow-up subscription solicitation that describes the newsletter, with a free copy, three months after the book has been bought — from you, which puts the mailing list in your control. And, beginning three to six months after the book is offered for sale, you will run ads about it in the professional publications sent to dentists.

Let's say that if 12,500 dentists buy the book, then 6,250 might subscribe to the newsletter: some would be book buyers, others attracted by the display ads in the journals. If it costs $49 a year for the newsletter and $12/year for you to produce and mail, plus $30,000 is set aside for promotional expenses, that would result in an additional income of $200,000 a year.

The book, in this instance, first explains the new concept, then says that for future, continual updating readers should become newsletter subscribers.

But once the book has been sold out, the newsletter performs the function of explaining the concept to future dentists as well as those who did not purchase the book when it was available, and it keeps related information current for all subscribers. That is, after the book is unavailable one would simply subscribe to the newsletter. This should result in a steadily increasing subscription total. Let me estimate that at $50,000 additional profit (from about 1,900 new subscriptions, or 1.5% of the total dentists) for each of the second through the fifth year, an annual newsletter will ultimately bring an income of some $400,000, and conceivably much more.

OTHER, SIMILAR BOOKS

Even though you know insurance for dentists best, there is no reason to stop with that vocation. Could you explain how malpractice premiums in other fields could be reduced by a similar amount? And would gynecologists, chiropractors, lawyers, physical therapists, or neurosurgeons, for example, be any less eager to spend $20 to find out how to save thousands on a pay-ment they already dislike?

To do that you set up the "Lower Malpractice Insurance Premium Publishing Company," with you as the publisher. You list all of the vocations, sub-practices, and branches that require malpractice insurance; you hire a competent writer for each field to produce a book that follows the format created in *Dentists: How to Lower Your Malpractice Insurance Premiums 50%*; and you promote each of these books in roughly the same way.

Your profits should be about the same, minus 10% for the writer — plus a huge bonus for producing a good book: the edi-torship and 35% of the list price of the resulting newsletters sold to those clients.

How much profit would you realize from these books? Let's say you publish only six to a total market of 350,000. Figuring three flyers for a dollar to contact the potential buyers, $2 to pro-duce and print each book, and for the $19.95 list price another $2 royalty to the writer at a 10% sales ratio, your profit would be about $400,000, after deducting some $40,000 for overhead for the now expanding firm.

And if the practitioners in each of these markets, starting three to six months after their respective book flyers have been distributed, began subscribing to a newsletter for $49 (but which again costs you $12 a year to produce and mail), to an initial 5% selling ratio that would increase 25% of that 5% for each of the next four years, how much might that bring, after deducting 35% of the gross income for the writer and setting aside $90,000 an-nually for promotion and additional overhead? $257,375 the first year, $344,219 the second, and so on....

If you are thinking of quitting this windfall after three years you should have realized profits of $180,000 for your initial book concerning dentists and malpractice insurance; $200,000 from the newsletter the first year; $250,000 the second; another $400,000 from the six formatted books to other malpractice-prone professions; $257,375 from newsletters to these latter six mar-kets, and $344,219 the next year. Or $1,231,594. If you'd wait a year longer that would be $1,962,657.

Not included is income from other information dissemina-tion means, such as articles, talks, speeches, seminars, audio or videocassettes, consulting, even the sale of insurance itself.

And the above figures could result in far more (or less) in-come with simple adjustments. Raise the book's cost to $24.95

and you earn $311,759 more. Lower the newsletter to $44.95 and you lose $96,187 (but recoup $24,806 from the writers' 35% bonus). If the book includes color on its pages or a fancy cover and costs $4 a copy to produce and print, you lose $95,000. Lower the writer's bonus on the newsletter to 25% and your profits increase $85,750 the first year and $21,440 more each year thereafter. Or should the postal rates and flyer design and printing costs reduce your flyer cost/mailing ratio from 3 for $1 to 2.5 for $1 you will lose $31,634 in the initial promotion of your seven books.

One can get lost in the figures, as important as they are. What I've tried to show here is that indispensability, immortality (of a terrestrial sort) and wealth are readily accessible to those willing to work to create them.

The rest of this book shows how to do it.

"The ideas I stand for are not mine. I borrowed them from Socrates. I swiped them from Chesterfield. I stole them from Jesus. And I put them in a book. If you don't like their rules, whose would you use?"

Dale Carnegie, *Newsweek* (1955)

To live in the hearts we leave behind,
Is not to die.

Thomas Campbell (1777-1844)

Chapter 2

Selling Special Information

You sell information to become indispensable, immortal, and rich.

Certain kinds of information in certain ways.

Telling others how to speak a language that has neither structure nor purpose, other than that you invented it, will not make you rich. Telling them how to wiggle their noses will not make you indispensable or immortal.

But telling fast food restaurant owners how their over-the-counter salesfolk can increase a restaurant's net income 30% by employing six tested techniques will indeed make you, to them, indispensable and slightly immortal — and rich. 60%, more so. 100%, much more so!

So any kind of information won't do.

It has to have value to the buyer well beyond what it costs to receive, in both time and expense.

If it costs the honchos of the fast food salesfolk the equivalent of 40% net income to learn how to save 30%, why would they buy it? Or if it took so long to hear, was so difficult to comprehend, or had to go through several translators, and in effect cost more than it would save, the old system won't be changed and you won't be heard, read, or paid.

Conversely, if you want to tell brain surgeons how to remove blood clots quicker and better, they might be receptive. But if you must first become a brain surgeon — and you're now a tree surgeon, — to create and convey that message would cost far more than it could ever return, however meritorious your intent.

The information you can sell to become indispensable, immortal, and wealthy must be valuable, unique, fully understandable, properly positioned, and conveyable in an acceptable marketing way.

It can be new information, old information presented in a new or different manner, or combinations of old and old or new information presented in a new or different way.

Value is determined by the buyer. Your contribution must have sufficient worth to justify the time, expense, and energy the buyer expends to comprehend (and often apply) it. Its worth must also be high enough to motivate the buyer to make its purchase.

Uniqueness in this sense means that the information is different from other information otherwise available — or is presented in a different fashion, is more accessible, or is more applicable. Singular is a synonym that also comes to mind.

Fully comprehensible is. So must be the information you sell.

Properly positioned refers to the buyer's mind-set and the information offered. It must be explained in such a way that it fits into the buyer's understanding of the general subject and need. Telling shepherds how to flange aluminum is like explaining wool carding to a plumber or poet: a mismatch, however well done. But telling printers how a new press will increase the speed of their print run twofold is information properly positioned. It fits into the buyer's broad scope of expertise and meets a need.

Finally, being conveyable in an acceptable marketing way simply means that you can profitably share that information by means that are used, effective, and understandable. Telling others how to cook pot roast could be done through a cookbook, a workshop or cooking demonstration, or even by videocassette. But it can't be done with semaphore flags or, easily, by singing or painting.

To get beyond these definitions we must now add another element. In this context, the information is intimately related to the needs of its buyer.

So let's switch to the process in the next chapter, talk about targeting, find a buyer, and from there zero in on the kind of information, the subject, that will bring you indispensability, immortality, and wealth.

Chapter 3

Finding Your Marketing Target

In *Self-Publishing to Tightly-Targeted Markets* I use three letters to describe a process applicable to niche marketing: T.C.E., which stand for targeting, customizing, and expanding.

Let me build on that same theme in this book, borrowing those same letters, in that order, and the core of that process but expanding it well beyond self-publishing in both how it is applied and when.

Let's explore the "T" for targeting first. Without knowing who your clients are, why, and how you can meet at least one of their vital needs, meeting your goals is likely to be, at best, serendipitous.

That word is well chosen. "Serendipity" refers to an aptitude for making fortunate discoveries accidentally. Almost the reverse of what is required to succeed as this book proposes. Our system requires a hard-edged purpose, no-nonsense determination to achieve it, skills applied with that purpose and achievement in mind — and proper speed a factor at every step. (Though we'll naturally accept some serendipity too.)

You become indispensable, immortal, and rich by selling information. But that information must help others. So you must know what kind of help they need.

Yet before knowing that you must know who those others are. Particularly since you'll spend a fair amount of your working life with them.

The blessing here is that you can choose the people you want to help. If helping cannibals makes you queasy, look elsewhere. If the thought of helping solve soothsayers' woes appalls, don't. First find a group or kind of people you care about, want to help succeed, and like being with. Or many groups or kinds, and select one to help first.

Alas, not all target markets are equal. Some are too small, others are too scattered, others seem to exist solely to resist help, and others — lovely nonetheless — haven't a spare ruble to pay for help. All of that is important because to meet your goals your market must eagerly want to pay you for your succor and if there are too few of them or they are too widely or loosely scattered that target market just won't work for you.

Step 1, then, is to determine your target market. Specifically, whom do you want to rub elbows with, get to know intimately, care deeply about, want to see prospering and growing as quickly as you are? Don't worry about how you're going to help them get there. Now just give them a name that you could find in some index: cosmetologists, accountants, female cab drivers, golfers over 40, gay novelists, social workers, chocolate addicts, secretaries....

Step 2, qualify this list. Accepting the fact that, unless you purposely hunt for the reverse, any target market is mostly composed of good, honorable, loving people, and some markets nonetheless aren't conducive to helping you achieve your goals. To eliminate them before spending unprofitable time and energy, these are the questions you must ask:

(1) Are there enough people in this target market?
(2) Do they care enough about their needs to want them met?
(3) Will they pay enough to meet them?
(4) Are they sufficiently accessible for you to be able to inform them about your services and for them to respond to your assistance?

Step 3, define and list their most critical needs, then select one to use as the core of your program.

We will develop these three steps in Chapter 5.

But first we must define the single most important question, "Why do you want to get rich?" Indispensability isn't the prime issue, rather a way to achieve that wealth faster and more easily. Immortality is a relative thing that, in fact, one can't achieve physically and nobody can prove religiously, so it's simply a way here of saying that you might be around at least in memory for somebody's grandchildren's grandchildren to honor.

But being rich is tangible and it needn't be in currency. Of the three it is the strongest motivator. So we need to know now, before you get too involved in the rest of the process, why you want that wealth. What are your dreams? How does this figure into your life plan?

If you don't know, where are you going to find the strength and direction that will keep you on course? Without a life path, why do you bother to even begin this shorter trek? For to succeed as I am proposing isn't a stroll in the park, it's a near-vertical climb on a mostly uncharted mountain, high in personal risk and subject at every step to failure.

Let's talk about that in the next chapter.

"We are all, it seems, saving ourselves for the Senior Prom. But many of us forget that somewhere along the way we must learn to dance."

Alan Harrington, *Life in the Crystal Palace* (1959)

Chapter 4

... After Finding Yourself

When I used to read or hear people asking invasive questions like "Why do *you* want to get rich?" my hackles would rise — at least I think they were my hackles. My instant reaction was to shout back, "What's it to you? Why do *you* like asking such stupid questions?"

I was partly right: whose business is it anyway?

But I was mostly wrong — and overly sensitive for the wrong reasons. A few years of maturity, or perhaps a bit more common sense, would have told me that it wasn't the answer to the question that was being sought that bothered me, but whether I had ever thought that answer through, whatever it was. Because without thinking it through I probably would never get what I sought: in this case, to be rich.

So let me say up front that I don't care why you want the money, unless you plan to give it to me! It is to be your money to use as you wish: to endow a bed at an orphanage, put your kids through barber school, buy furniture, island hop, stuff in your sofa, ...

But I do care very much that you know *why* you want to get rich because in that knowing comes most of the fuel to make it happen. The two most important elements to achieving success, in my mind, are desire and persistence. Knowing why provokes the desire and gives backbone to the persistence.

Therefore we must step back here, ask some larger questions about you and life in general, then see where this part of it fits in.

For example, how do you want to be remembered by your grandchildren? What kind of impact do you want to have or what contribution do you want to make with this life? What specific achievement(s) would make your existence worthwhile?

I prefer a three-pronged life-planning approach. The first prong asks what kind of life, in general, do you want to lead on earth?

The second asks where you want to be, precisely, in five years: job, position, income, equity, expenses, marital status, children, reputation, other assets.

And the third asks what you must do, in very specific terms, during the first, second, third, and fourth years to achieve that fifth-year position while leading the kind of life you wish on earth.

It's important to know how an 18-month, no-holds lunge at indispensability, immortality, and wealth will alter your life plan! So if no such life plan exists, let's create one now.

The first prong is easy enough to create on paper. In response to the question about the kind of life you want to lead on earth, make a list of what you want to achieve in the broadest sense (happiness, security, a comfortable home, health,...) and the kind of person you want to be (stern, honest, loving, exact,...) as you realize those achievements.

Those are the achievement highways and the behavioral and emotional paths that lead you to being the kind of person you wish.

Good enough, but broad achievements and being a good person are the results of a thousand lesser acts — sharp decisions, hard work, fairness and attention to detail and letting others know that you are posed to help, in short the breaking down of global dreams into exact goals. The latter require more attention, more thought, modification, and just plain enactment.

Which is why a detailed, complete five-year plan and a series of firm yet flexible plans, one each from the first to fourth year, are needed, as a measuring tool for the past and future while the major plan reaches fulfillment.

I describe such a process in *Empire-Building by Writing and Speaking*, and justify the myriad of integrated steps "because the total picture cannot be painted without all of the colors. Life is always in harmony, and to live it fully you must know, as best you can, what you are seeking and why, to synchronize the harmony of your objective with the greater reality."

What do you do now? Put the first prong down in writing: the kind of life you want to lead and the kind of person you want to be. Spend time here. Paint the true you in acts and person, as you want to be and are willing to work to become.

Then develop the full fifth-year portrait of yourself, as you wish to be, precisely, at that time: job, position, income, equity, expenses, marital status, children, reputation, other assets. Again, on paper, with close attention to detail.

Now sketch out roughly where you want to be at each of the four anniversary markers, particularly concerning income and equity, since this book talks about making money.

Then let's hold the shorter goals and means of achieving them in suspension until you've read the rest of the book and can calculate how the adaptation of its message might be integrated into all three prongs: your larger life style and purpose, your fifth-year goal, and the measuring dates between now and then.

Let's return to your personal targets later, in Chapter 12, after we're shared more process.

"It has always been like writing a check.... It is easy to write a check if you have enough money in the bank, and writing comes more easily if you have something to say."

Sholem Asch, *New York Herald Tribune* (1955)

Chapter 5

Qualifying and Nichifying Your Market

Once you know why you want the money and how its pursuit fits into your greater life plan, the next step is getting it.

The single most important thing in niche marketing is identifying the niche, that is, finding your target market, qualifying it, and determining what that market cares enough about to make you rich providing it.

So here let's flesh out the three steps introduced in the third chapter.

Step 1 was to determine your target market and give it a name.

Since you can choose the people you want to help — you can be a niche picker — why not pick the kind that you enjoy being with and truly want to see succeed, because as they succeed so will you. Done right, you will soon be mixing in their milieu many hours a day, most days of the week, for years. It's your life. Why not people it with elbow-rubbers of choice?

That's it. Make a list — this book is long on list-making, then doing something with it! List every kind of person, vocation, group, hobbyist, specialist, fan, sex (not too many of those), ethnic member, nationality,... Then rank them in the order in which you'd like to meet their needs. We will concentrate on your top three selections in Step 2.

Step 2 says that not everybody listed can or will bring you the degree of financial return we discuss in this book. (If that's unimportant to you, fine. Provide a replacement motivation and reward, continue, and read what I say about wealth with the proper bemusement.) To weed out the less remunerative we must qualify your list.

NUMERICAL QUALIFICATION

The first form of qualification is numerical. Are there enough people in this market to reward you sufficiently?

A check with a reference librarian will usually lead you to the current count of practitioners in your chosen fields.

Or a telephone call to the appropriate trade or professional association offices, or similar servicing bodies if they exist, will often get the same results. Phone numbers and addresses can be found in the *Directory of Associations* in most libraries. Be certain, though, that you have the total number of people in the field and not just those who are members.

A third method dovetails with a later concern in Step 2, the target market's accessibility, which usually means how easily you can reach them by mail. A way to complete both hunts simultaneously is to check the number of people in the field in the *Standard Rate and Data Services Mailing Lists* publications.

How many is enough? How tall is tall? I suppose it matters where you're looking from — or, in niche marketing, how much money you want to earn and by which means.

In the opening chapter we offered a rough example that began with a book called *Dentists: How to Lower Your Malpractice Insurance Premiums 50%*. In that case there were 125,000 accessible in the field, the book cost $19.95, and a profit of $180,000 was anticipated.

Let me offer a standard example from a different perspective, though the number/cost/profit ratios are in the same proportion.

To earn approximately $50,000 profit from a niche-marketed book you need to sell a $15 book to roughly 67,000 people — and earn a 50% profit from each sale.

So if $50,000 profit is acceptable, you need about 67,000 in your target market. But if each book sells for $30 you need only half as many. If it sells for $7.95, twice as many (or 134,000) — the same number you would need if only 5% of your market bought it.

In other words, using the standard example as a base for a book, you can relatively manipulate the other numbers.

So if your market penetration is to be by book at the outset, a market of redheaded Norwegian-speaking llama herders (maybe two worldwide, if you could find them) won't work. But redheads (there are millions of them) would.

What numbers do you need if you plan to penetrate using other means?

Articles alone will never bring the financial return you seek, however large the number.

Newsletters are excellent tools once your expertise in a field is broadly recognized — usually through articles, a book, or some form of speaking. So they aren't normally a means of consideration at the outset.

Audio and video tapes for niche markets are sold much like books so the number is directly related to the cost of the item, the percentage of the market that will buy it, and what percentage of that income will be profit. Inserting those numbers into the standard example will give you a target market size.

Besides books, speeches and seminars are usually the best lead items to establish your expertise and to utilize for the subsequent sale of more related information.

Niche topic speeches are almost always given to gathered segments of your target market, such as meetings of association members, employees, clubs, or other similar congregations. The question is less the global size of the number of the target market than its organization and desire to pay you to speak.

Seminars, on the other hand, can be a particularly good way to show your expertise and to sell information. They can be offered much like speeches, through neutral sponsorship like universities and extended education programs, to businesses or corporations, or you may sponsor them yourself.

The "best" size for your target market in this case is determined by how much you charge for the seminar, how much its presentation costs you (for the site, help, handout materials, refreshments, travel, room/board, and so on), how much of that is profit, and how much it costs to get the participants to register and attend.

Seminar target markets can be smaller than those required to profit from books because, once you have identified those most eager to participate and convinced them that your message is worth hearing, you can easily develop and offer closely related presentations that they also need or want to know. Since the product is oral and thus infinitely malleable, only the workbook production and promotion must be adjusted for each new presentation.

In short, I can't tell you with the same degree of certainty for the other means how many people you need to get rich. A gut feeling tells me that if a market is big enough for a book to create gold, alchemy by other means should also succeed.

QUALIFICATION BY DESIRE

Do the people in your target market care enough about their needs to want them met? That's hard to measure subjectively on a general level.

Some target markets are so loosely held together and the bonds are so ephemeral that it's hard to tell what those needs even are.

Chocolate lovers are a viable niche market. Surely they would be elated with ever-better tasting chocolate instantly accessible at rock-bottom prices, if not free. But realistically, they'd gleefully settle for any of the three, and probably not burn down City Hall if even one were impossible. Nor would they probably pay much money to make it so.

On the other hand, have chocolate abolished or taxed out of reason and even a marginal target market in terms of need suddenly becomes an area where a niche solution finds a problem worth the expense to get solved.

So that becomes the nub, the measurement by which we can qualify by desire. Will the target market pay enough to meet both its need and yours? Do they care enough about both their problem and your solution to gladly (if unknowingly) thrust you toward a six-figure income in 18 months? If so, they qualify!

In Step 3 we will see how you ferret out just such a solution to virtually assure that the requisite desire exists to ease their pain while fueling your pleasure.

QUALIFICATION BY MONEY

If one of your goals is to reach a specific level of income, or even a general level of affluence, through niche marketing, it is important to know whether your target market has or can get the funds to pay you, the desire or will power to do so, and when.

Some worthy markets live outside the moneyed market; others are on the fringe. Yet neither should be summarily disqualified.

If your goal is to teach guinea pig raising to the poorest tribe in eastern Ecuador, that is admirable. Guinea pigs breed quickly, grow fast, and taste good. But if you hope to earn $50,000 annually through this venture, the tribe can't come close to meeting your hope however much it may wish to or however many piglets it consumes.

Sometimes creative thinking can turn seemingly impossible economic situations into a double-win reality. Establishing an institute for the worldwide propagation, distribution, and consumption of guinea pigs might well propel you toward your goal and allow you not only to help that tribe in Ecuador but hundreds of other groups across the globe.

How do you know if a target market will pay for your product or services? Study their buying practices: how do they spend their money, where, and for what? If what they buy resembles what you sell for about the same cost, that's a good sign.

But if doubt still lingers, ask if what you want to sell them is sufficiently important for them to buy. Literally ask a representative cross-section of them with a questionnaire, a survey, or one-on-one. Better to ask now than to make assumptions, invest heavily, and discover that what you see as mankind's salvation just makes others scratch their heads and stare.

QUALIFICATION BY ACCESSIBILITY

You have to reach a niche market to help it. No reach or no help, no money for you!

Yet accessibility works two ways. Your market must be accessible to you to help; your message convincing them of their need and that you can meet or solve it must, also, be accessible.

One example of the latter concerns language. If the inhabitants of a remote settlement in China are dying from eating a favorite plant and you discover a simple and inexpensive chemical solution that converts the toxin in that plant into needed protein, they would gratefully buy and sprinkle your cure on their favorite dish. But if you advertise in English and send Croatian-speaking salesfolk to extol its wonders in that tongue, the information is inaccessible in roughly the same way it would be if you couldn't find your market, it was too scattered, or there were no way to put your message, in the proper tongue, before it.

Usually, though, accessibility refers to the physical means of contacting the target market. And in most cases the best way to do that is by mail. Not a broadsheet to anybody but a flyer prepared and directed precisely to those members of your niche market about the subject in question. Not a brochure telling anybody how to bond two new plastic forms of piping but a detailed, specific how-to brochure to plumbers who use plastic piping, with a full explanation of how your product makes this act the best thing to do, plus easy and fast to use, reliable, and inexpensive.

The key, then, is finding a mailing list to your specific target market, one that is, like the bond, easy and fast to use, reliable, and inexpensive — and current.

Fortunately, it is relatively easy to find out if your target market is accessible by mail. Most larger libraries subscribe to the *Standard Rate and Data Services Mailing Lists* publications which, once you figure out its labyrinthine organization, can show you which lists exist, their cost, the form in which they can be obtained (usually Cheshire format, on magnetic tape, or pressure-sensitive labels), how they are gathered, where those listed come from (by ZIP or state), when they were last cleaned, and other valuable data.

Most lists appear on those pages. But one can also ask the various groups, associations, publications, newsletters, card deck distributors, and others dealing with your target market whether they have lists for rent or if they know of lists that you can check for possible use.

Let's say that you have completed steps one and two. You know your target market, it is sufficiently large, its members care very much about meeting their needs and are eager to pay a reasonable amount to do so, and they are accessible by several good, clean mailing lists.

What is missing is to find that core topic, that one critical need that these people want desperately to solve and that you want as keenly to help them do so. In other words, that topic where their need and your desire felicitously intersect, where their happiness and yours come from your acquiring and sharing expertise about something you enjoy.

Which brings us to Step 3: defining and listing your target market's most critical needs, then selecting one to use as the core of your program. Time to go for the jugular. Ask yourself where your market's desire for change is the greatest. What would they pay the most to know the quickest?

Write down every answer that comes from this question: "What problems, frustrations, hopes, and dreams does my target market have?" If you gave them magic powder, how would they use it? If you could grant them a miracle, what would it be? Write down anything that comes to mind.

Note that we're going for the throat. For a six-figure base in 18 months you need courage at every step. No step is more important than the picking of the core topic upon which you will build your niche empire.

The best way to find out about the market's problems, frustrations, sought-for miracles, and dreams is to ask those in it. Circulars, opinion polls, one-on-one investigation. Nothing will bring better results if you ask the right question(s).

Take those responses, lump them into need categories, and prioritize them. Then look at that top category and ask what is the vital thread that holds that group together: what is the core topic that desperately needs a fast, workable reply? That is the heart of your success. Pose that need in an universally recognizable form, offer one or many applicable solutions, and build outward from there.

If your topic is one that the target market members think about once a year, in passing, that's either a weak topic or an indifferent market. You're not close to their top priority. Why would they pay you to know what you know?

But if your theme is on the cutting edge, vitally affects the income and self-worth of everyone in the field, and they are frantically awaiting the arrival of a savior to lead them through the forest, then you must get your help to them as fast as possible! You are at the heart of their greatest need, they want help, and they will pay — sometimes hugely — for it.

This element of niche marketing is too critical to leave here. Everything depends upon the topic you select. So let's dedicate the next chapter to looking at 100 niche marketing ideas or topics. Something you are about to read may be the basestone to the foundation of your fortune. Or will suggest an idea that has been hiding in a remote brain lobe and needed pecuniary prodding. Anyway, seeing 100 more ways to get to your gilded Rome won't hurt.

Chapter 6

100 Niche Marketing Ideas

A few years back I prepared a report called "100 Topics for Niche Marketed Books" as a follow-up to my book *Self-Publishing to Tightly-Targeted Markets.*

In what follows I am drawing heavily from that report for two reasons: one, I received many grateful responses to it from wanna-be niche book publishers who couldn't for the life of them think of a topic or title, and two, it was prepared with this book in mind, to be used just about here. That is why what follows is plagiarized from me.

First, there is the most obvious kind of niche marketed topic. Let's use nursing here as an example.

(1) "How does one become a nurse?" (The precise steps, from schooling through hiring.)

Then, (2) "How does one become unfirable as a nurse?"

Or what about these basic spinoffs related to the position itself?

(3) "What 10 steps (or 5, 15, or 50) make every nurse excel?"
(4) "Where do you go from nursing — and what can you do while nursing that will get you there as quickly and profitably as possible?"
(5) "How do you use your job as a nurse to move directly to the top of your field?"

What do nurses — or those so aspiring — want to know? These are the core questions one simply must ask in order to excel. (Focus on people who want to go to the top, move ahead, make a mark, become exceptional: they will buy your information because they want to progress quickly and surely. To do that they have learned to listen to experts. So you sell core information packed for easy comprehension and quick application. Forget the plodders. Anybody can plod free of charge.)

Focusing on how one uses that job to create an even better life gives us:

(6) "How do you use your job as a nurse to create financial security, which you can then parlay into true wealth?"
(7) "How can nurses maximize their basic and fringe benefits: health insurance, Keogh plan, illness or injury protection, others...?"
(8) "How does being a nurse provide a launching pad to change (the world, society, the town, children's welfare, etc.)?"

Many niche fields, like nursing, require considerable learning and training. Thus additional key niche information suggests itself: (9) "Directory of the nursing schools in the U.S.: strengths, weaknesses, cost, and registration requirements."

(10) "Directory of programs and schools for specialized nurses, by category, cost, and registration requirements."

Practitioners of some niche fields such as nursing are particularly sought nationwide, even worldwide. In that case, (11) "A guide to nursing employment and employment services for placement throughout the (United States, Australia, English-speaking world, world, etc.)"

There is nothing more exciting than reading the words of people in your niche field describing what they do best and how they do it. That's a niche book (12): a collection of sharp articles or interviews from the best in the field.

On the other hand, a book of horror stories of the worst practitioners in nursing or most other niche field would be quickly bought. Book (13).

Here let's change the focus a bit. Let's presume that the buyer of your niche marketed information already is a _____. Say, "a home-based, self-employed computer operator," which we will abbreviate to a "C.O." Then a series of new questions opens up, each sufficiently important to warrant buying new information to answer them. For example...

(14) "How do you create enough new computer-related business, at the outset and continually once you are established, to reach your business goals?"

(15) "How do C.O.s create realistic, profitable mission goals and business plans — a step-by-step guide through the thought, planning, research, writing, editing, and final verification process?"

(16) "How can C.O.s double their incomes in one year without drastically altering their equipment or personnel needs?"

(17) "How do new C.O.s most economically and efficiently equip their offices — the basic equipment needs, where machinery and supplies can be found (with quality and cost in mind), how they can best be arranged, how long they can be expected to last, and how one can then save time and money on their replacement?"

(18) "How and where can the profitable C.O. find the best personnel — and what is more sensibly subcontracted out?"

(19) By extension, "How do you find the best subcontractors, and how do you assure that they perform as they promise?"

(20) "What kinds of employment contracts — if any — work best for C.O.s?" Describe the best and provide a sample.

(21) Create a book, a series of reports, or as the purpose of a newsletter case studies of good employment contracts: examples of actual contracts, with comments and suggestions.

(22) "Are model employment instruction programs needed? What kind of programs give the best results? How can the C.O. create or find and schedule them?"

In the beginning most businessfolk must keep their own accounting books, at least for tax purposes, and have little knowledge of how to do so. So information you sell is (23) "How to keep simple, straightforward, legal accounting records for C.O.s."

The follow-up information then becomes (24) "How to find, hire, maintain, and best utilize an outside accountant — and how you know when it's necessary."

Sometimes niche folk want to use their skill, talent, or knowledge in a different setting. So you explain (25) "How to use what you know about computer operations to relocate, personally or professionally."

And others might want to make the changes abroad, so (26) the appropriate explanation for them would be "How to use what you know about computer operations to move abroad!"

Often people in a niche field are eager to find others with whom to associate. So (27) a "Directory of _____ (people in the niche field)" would be a hot seller, if it includes addresses, phone and FAX numbers, and probably a bit more about each individual.

Niche people have a way of magnetically attracting others who want to or will service them, the way that artists attract canvas and paint sellers. So a broader kind of directory, a (28) "Directory of Needed Supplies, Services, and Consultants," with the title molded to match the field. These are done two ways: you list the folks free and charge the niche buyers to get to the information or you make those listed pay, produce the directory free or very inexpensively, and distribute it widely.

Another way of finding like souls in a niche field is to join appropriate association(s). As mentioned earlier, check the *Encyclopedia of Associations* in your library. Sometimes there is only one such association. But often there are many. In the latter case information that might come in handy for the newcomer would be (29) "The best associations for the _____ — and why!" Presumably you'd give full information about every related association, how one contacts them, the cost, and a detailed explanation of exactly why a person would join one or all, in some order of importance. Added to this might be the publications and services available from each, with annotations or commentary.

Labor unions are involved with some niche professions or fields, so (30) "Labor unions and the _____" might be quickly sought by those new to the field.

(31) "The C.O. and the I.R.S." Given that you want your buyers to be law-abiding and meet their taxpaying obligations, what philosophy and actions will nonetheless allow them to take all of the legal deductions possible? Best to include one or several plans, with tax forms as submitted and the rationale behind each C.O.-related action or deduction.

(32) Again, a compilation of federal tax case studies would be appreciated and widely used: give specific examples in full detail, with comments and suggestions.

(33) That compilation would presumably be composed of studies selected over the years that touch the widest range of in-

terest for C.O.s. You might offer another kind of compilation, produced annually, of federal tax cases of the previous year that affect only C.O.s.

(34) And still another, annual or biennial, of state tax cases affecting C.O.s.

(35) "The C.O. and the Law." Tell what every C.O. needs to know to operate legally both in the United States and their particular state, plus what pertinent local laws usually prevail in most communities. Include how and when it would be best to consult lawyers, how to find legal help knowledgeable about their field, and how they can find out about changes in the law that directly affect them.

(36) You guessed it: follow-up information about legal case studies concerning C.O.s, with the usual comments and suggestions.

(37) And why not an annual (or even a quarterly) newsletter of current cases affecting C.O.s, updating their progress and disposition over time, with comments and suggestions as appropriate to how these might affect the C.O.s reading those words?

(38) The previous two suggestions might be divided into different formats touching the federal courts and the state/local courts. Do C.O.s need legal contracts to conduct their business? Then try (39) "Fifteen (you pick the number) legal contracts for C.O.s," probably best presented in book or computer disk form.

Let's take a breather for a moment and discuss the underlying philosophy that makes each of these ideas convertible to almost every field. It is that very little accessible information of a current, accurate, specific nature exists in most fields today. And practitioners in those fields are starved for it, can't find it, and will pay well to get it.

Moreover, it is far easier to find information now. One, you can comb the printed material: books, articles, newsletters, case studies, court cases, whatever. Two, you can do that from your home or office rather than solely in person, through computer databases and library holdings that you reach by machine. Finally, people are usually the best source of what you need to know now. Your best research tool is often the phone or FAX. More on this in the next chapter when we discuss establishing and solidifying your expertise. It's enough now to know that niche marketing presumes something to sell, and what better than vital information those in that niche need to know but can't find — or don't trust.

Let's switch focus from the C.O.s for whom there is very little in print to another field which is rich in literature. That creates different opportunities for your niche marketing.

For example, (40) create a bibliography of the articles or books of general or specific interest to your niche readers, preferably annotated and in order of value.

By extension, consider (41) other specific, annotated bibliographies: audio or videocassettes, newsletters, films, and other forms of information dissemination.

Some practitioners new to a field are vaguely aware of the choice of current periodicals, newsletters, and other printed information sources, so you might (42) either list everything currently available in the field, with comments as to its value, applicability, and how it can be ordered/subscribed to, or you can (43) set up "the ideal reading/listening/viewing schedule" for a practitioner, with the above details plus an estimate of which item is the most important (and why), the relative time ratio you would suggest for each item noted, and perhaps even some thoughts on how this reading, listening, or viewing might best be integrated into a busy schedule.

Also, why not create (44) an anthology where, rather than refer the reader to a bibliography, you select the best works and reprint or reproduce them either in their entirety or in abridged form, with or without editorial comments, footnotes, or updates? Remember to follow the copyright laws here.

Or (45) develop many anthologies, each created by a special criterion: by date ("Works about _____ in the 1920's,""...1930's," etc.), by topic category, by political orientation, by sex, and so on....

On the other hand, some folks in your niche field may be interested in creating some of that literature — that is, they may want to write, speak, or produce viewing material. While some will want to do this about subjects outside the niche field, let's focus here on the niche topic and how you can help them serve it.

(46) You might tell them "How to publish magazine articles about _____ (the niche topic)," showing those interested how they can establish their expertise and share knowledge with col-

leagues in the professional journals in the field. Explain both the process and how to find the most appropriate markets, with details.

(47) Sometimes they'd rather attract customers by more publicly displaying their expertise, which means articles to general magazines and newspapers. So here the title would be "How to publish articles about _____ (the niche topic) to be read by potential customers!" (Since my expertise is information dissemination by writing and speaking, let me suggest a few of my own works that would help you help others in these areas. Here my *How to Sell More Than 75% of Your Freelance Writing* and *The Writer's Guide to Query Letters & Cover Letters* would be excellent sources about the freelance article writing process.)

(48) Others will want to write a book in the field so you explain "How to write and publish books about _____ (the niche topic)."

There are other ways to share information about a niche topic than through books or articles.

(49) "How to produce and sell audiocassettes about _____." (We have a helpful 60-minute tape about just this subject that will provide the basics: *"Producing and Selling Your Own Audio Cassette."*)

(50) "How to produce and sell videocassettes about _____."

(51) "How to produce and market your own newsletter about _____."

(52) "How to set up and market your own seminar about _____." (As a guide, check our audiocassette series called, appropriately, *"How to Set Up and Market Your Own Seminar."*)

(53) "How to speak about _____ (the niche topic) and get paid for it!"

(54) "How to speak to potential customers about _____." And, finally, (55) "How to produce and sell (reports, case studies, etc.) about _____."

Don't forget that many niche folk know something that others will pay to learn directly, so telling them (56) "How to become a consultant about _____" should be popular.

Then (57) "How to build a _____ empire from consulting" might appeal, though it could as well be built from any of the information-dissemination means you use to display your expertise, like articles, books, tapes, or a newsletter. (Here our book *Empire-Building by Writing and Speaking* will provide guidance.)

Experts in a niche field usually want to share that expertise with others. There is a regular process by which you let media know that you are in fact an expert, up-to-date, and eager to speak about your topic. So:

(58) "How to share your expertise about _____ in the newspapers."
(59) "How to share your expertise about _____ on radio or TV."

Why not write a column? (60) "How to publish a column about _____ in newspapers and magazines."
Or have a radio/TV show? (61) "How to create and offer radio and TV programs about _____."

Another way to find a topic for a niche book is to juxtapose the field with either another field or a technology. Write out the niche topic and simply list other, related topics or technologies. Compare them. Sometimes they fit! For example:

(62) "Juggling for pay during the basketball (football, etc.) halftime break!"
(63) "Computers and the dental office."
(64) "Junk car jockeys and the museum."
(65) "Where and how chiropractors and osteopaths work in profitable harmony."

Then you must find examples and explain the ways!

Most niche areas are somehow customer-related thus promotion of the skill, trade, subject, or product is involved. Potential sales will get those in the niche field eager to buy your information. The kind you might write:

(66) "How to find eager customers for _____ (the niche field or a product or service from that field)."
(67) "Where to find and profitably use mailing lists to sell _____."
(68) "How to sell _____ at conventions, fairs, or local meetings."
(69) "How the clever use of promotional inserts about _____ can double your exposure and increase your profits." A counterpart niche offering might be (70) "How to create your own promotional inserts — or buy them 90% done!"

(71) "How to create a take-home flyer that will increase knowledge about and confidence in your (trade, practice, or profession) — and increase your customer load!"

(72) "Debunk the myths: creating your own flyer that brings in customers by driving out the lies!"

Folks often want to learn more about their niche field while traveling in North America or overseas. Why not provide information about just that, like (73) "How to learn more about _____ while traveling in the U.S. and Canada?"

Or (74) "How to learn more about _____ while traveling in (Chile, Europe, the Near East, London)."

Think of selling niche information from the desired result first. Why will people pay to buy information about a particular subject? Because they want to achieve something through that subject, like success, happiness, uniqueness, big money....

Thus four topics immediately suggest themselves, plus one more for every additional high-benefit desire you can think of.

(75) "How to achieve success in _____," which can be hyped by adding in "extraordinary" before success — or quantify the process, such as "Ten steps to success in _____."

(76) "How to achieve happiness in _____." Eternal happiness?

(77) "How to achieve uniqueness in _____." Kind of vague. Why not "How to become the world's best in _____."? Maybe Cook County's best?

(78) And "How to make BIG MONEY in _____." What makes a bigger splash is citing an amount of big money that one can realistically earn — then explain how. Like $50,000 or $100,000 or even $1,000,000. Avoid specific numbers, like $37,186. People will think it's a joke and not buy the information. Really.

These four provoke some spinoffs. One applies here and to almost all of the rest of the 100 niche book ideas: combine ideas by linking (75) and (76) you get (79) "How to achieve success and happiness in _____." Or (80) "How to achieve success and happiness in _____ by earning an extra $200,000!"

There are dozens of approaches to that idea in most niche fields. If the niche field you are serving is that of dollhouse builders, (81) "How to build dollhouses might become (82) "How to become the world's best dollhouse builder." But tighten the definition more and you can write something like (83) "How to become the world's best wooden (or plastic, metal, prefab, Victorian, etc.) dollhouse builder." Or (84) "How to be the world's best miniature Georgian dollhouse builder," by combining specialties.

Many niche fields have seasonal variations. From that might come:

(85) "A seasonal flow chart (or calendar) of _____ (niche field) activities."
(86) "A seasonal promotional calendar for _____ activities."

It needn't be seasonal and the book could contain both. Such as (87) "A promotional calendar and flow chart for _____ activities."

And what about the off-season? The ski instructor sans snow or the tax person in October. So the book might be (88) "How to use your _____ (niche field) skills in the off-season!"
Or, leaving the seasonal slant, (89) "How to parlay interest in _____ (niche field) to other (fun, profitable) employment (or use, jobs, hobbies, contributions)."

Since many niche interests aren't economically oriented — volunteering at the elderhostel, grocery shopping for the bedbound, reading books at school — different kinds of book possibilities emerge:

(90) "Volunteering in _____ (niche field): how to maximize the use of your caring and skills." (Could range from how to improve the quality of what you do to where to find people or groups needing your skills.)
(91) "Volunteering and the I.R.S. — what is deductible, when, and how."
(92) "How to find more, eager volunteers in _____ — and what to do with them once you have them!"

A true twist: (93) use your interest in the niche field as the core or background for a novel. Then let those with a similar interest know that that is what the novel is all about!

Niche folk sometimes want to see something about the topic in print but are less interested in written explanation than in the visuals themselves, so (94) your book could be an illustration book of line art, diagrams, fort designs, battlefield maps, art designs, blueprints.

A step further: rather than line art only, yours is (95) a photo book, of blacks in the Civil War, Frank Lloyd Wright homes, every Chicago Cub annual team photo since 1876, red birds, ...

If the niche is invention-related, one can comb the patent office application files and produce something like (96) "_____ (niche topic) inventions since (the first year you find an example)." Include the text and art, with comments.

Great gifts to those with a niche-related passion are (97) joke books of every bit of humor you can find related to that field.

As salable are (98) cartoon books about the same niche field. (You can mix jokes and cartoons in the same book too!) Remember, when you are using others' works take care to check the "fair use" copyright laws!

Why not (99) documentary information about the field in general: from the beginning to now, definitive, the knowledge that every person with that passion must have?

Or the documentary can be broken into (100) historical or developmental periods, the latter usually divided into the phases of creation or production.

Sometimes the most interesting material comes from (101) comparisons, of the state-of-the-art in, say, the U.S. in the niche field and the (now former) Soviet Union. These can also be of earlier historical periods, different products from different developmental philosophies, even ideas in the common field of interest.

(102) State-of-the-art information itself is in high demand: where the niche field is today, in detail, plus where it may be in a year, two, and five.

Finally, why not (103) "The 10 most aggravating problems in _____ and how they can be solved"?
Or (104) "Ten predictions of where _____ will be in (10 years, the year 2000, next year)."

That's it! One hundred (plus four) topics for niche marketing. Some may be totally inappropriate for your market or your interests. Others are precisely what you can use. And many will suggest more ways you can approach your particular potential readership with other niche-based information.

I've just suggested 104 kinds of core topics.

Once you've found your own topic, ask yourself, "Do I want to devote the next two to three years to that subject? Do I really want to help the people in that market that much? Why? Why would I make that sacrifice? Why would I risk my money and energy that way?"

If you can't answer these questions with a ringing affirmation, if you're not fully committed, if there's some reservation in your honesty or conviction, either find another core topic or simply look elsewhere for your satisfaction. There's no shame or loss of face. Probably 99% of the people alive wouldn't be caught dead doing what this book proposes.

Yet if you're one of those extraordinary souls in that remaining 1% and everything you've read so far makes you tingle with anticipation, you can't wait to grapple with the core topic, and you know marrow-deep that niche marketing is where you want to be, welcome aboard. Next stop, chapter 7: becoming an expert.

Chapter 7

Becoming an Expert

You're not going to get rich in the kind of niche marketing I'm describing because you're good looking or tell rib-splitting jokes.

In fact most of those helping you get lifetime launched in 18 months will probably never see or hear you. To them you could be as ugly as a turkey's gobbler, talk like Big Bird, or be 105 years old. They don't care. They are buying information from you that they very much need and that they can't get elsewhere, or at least as readily, inexpensively, or as well explained.

They are buying your expertise. They'd prefer that you'd spent a lifetime gathering and experiencing the knowledge you're selling but even that is relatively unimportant. As long as it's accurate it can be minutes old and filtered through five people.

The pivotal word here is "expertise." That special knowledge or understanding that you have that they don't — or, sometimes, do but need validated.

So to niche market effectively you need something about which you are an expert to market to your niche. You have now defined that niche, know what its needs are, and which of those needs you are going to initially help it meet. That will get you out of first gear.

But it's not enough. What you also need is depth and breadth if you hope to spend a fruitful, rewarding time selling information because to do that you will almost certainly have to expand that core information and offer it, and its expanded components, by many means.

For example, I sell a report called "100 Best Travel Newspaper Markets." It has no value whatsoever to Auca Indians, helicopter pilots, or the criminally insane. But travel writers wanting to sell articles simultaneously to newspapers across the nation find both its reproducible format on Avery labels and $6 price a super bargain. Travel writers are my niche and my marketing pretty much consists of letting them know that the report exists.

I check with travel editors in August and we reissue a new version each September, so this bit of gathered information will continue to sell as long as we do our part and the writers need a new list. We are even considering giving them an option: in printed or computer disk format. Same information but two ways to access and use it.

Since I will never reach a six-figure income with this report you probably wonder why I'm wasting your time with such a petty and uninspiring example.

Because it is everything else that comes from or is directly related to that report that got me to that six-figure plateau, keeps me there, and provides my inspiration.

Here's the logic: Once I know that travel writers need to use those addresses I also know that they want and need to know how to sell simultaneously to newspapers with cover letters and singly through query letters to magazines, and how to sell reprints after the first magazine piece is in print. Which means that most of those buying that report will also gladly buy *The Travel Writer's Guide* and *The Writer's Guide to Query Letters & Cover Letters* because they contain that information. Also, most travel writers write in other fields and are as interested in selling their material in book form, so they will be nearly as eager to buy my writing books and reports about other formats and markets.

Writers also have ears! And they are enthusiastic about mixing with other writers, to see what they look like, learn new skills, and trade tips. So if travel writers will pay $6 to get the addresses of newspaper travel editors, many of them will also pay $45 to hear a no-nonsense four-hour, this-is-how-you-do-it seminar called "Writing Travel Articles That Sell!" — even though the essence of the process is in *The Travel Writer's Guide*. And many of those, writing about topics other than travel or wanting to know as much about the word-ordering process as the selling, will pay the same to hear seminars like "How to Sell 75% of Your Freelance Writing," "How to Research and Write Articles That Sell," and "Before You Write That Book...."

Yet not all travel writers live within my seminar-giving range nor can all attend on the date scheduled, so if the same program is captured on audiocassette, duplicates are made, and the same workbook is provided, with the resulting package costing about the same as the live presentation, those living a thousand miles away can avail themselves of the same material whenever they have the opportunity and desire to listen.

I can also speak to gatherings of writers about these or related subjects, or consult individually or collectively about writing things, or edit, or conceivably even publish. A newsletter would be possible, or many: one for travel writers, another for book writers, a third for ecology writers, and so on....

The point is: from a core need other needs become evident. Often those needs, like the core need, can be addressed by more than one means. From meeting that core need accurately, responsibly, fully, and in a manner that is easy to access, comprehend, and afford I have said to those in my niche market: I did it once, it worked, and I can do it again for related needs or by other means.

The market's response? It will buy as long as it continues to need every new information element I offer and the new material is, once more, accurate, responsible, and complete, plus easy to access, comprehend, and afford. Fail once and the market will be wary. Twice and it will almost certainly go elsewhere, if there is an elsewhere, or it will disappear.

The pivotal word is expertise. How do you create it? You work very, very hard.

Although in the beginning it's sometimes easy. Maybe you already know all there is to know about something unique. Or you can find something small but vital, zero in, learn everything you can learn about it, and sell a solution to a problem you have reminded your niche market that it has.

Then it gets tougher. You become a victim of your success. Those applying your solution, even those who don't apply it but know you suggested it and it works, recognize you as an expert in their field. They presume you have other workable solutions for other gnarly problems. They assume you are current on the literature, know what the other experts are saying, and can apply new thought to their old needs. In short, unless you flee the niche market you'd better become what they expect real quick!

And, odd as it sounds, that defines the kind of expert you must become. You learn everything you can about every pertinent aspect of your subject. You master its history, try all the experiments, know who said and did what, when, and why, become conversant on the operational processes, rebuild the crankshaft so often you can do it blindfolded in gardening gloves, cram on the jargon, know the basics and permutations cold.

Or you define specifically where your expertise is, draw boundaries, and stay safely within the ramparts.

It takes work. Books, articles, subscriptions to necessary journals, membership and participation in association(s), reading the card deck and mail order pamphlets, making topic computer searches in the library, whatever is needed to get all related information in your hands from the past, now, and as it breaks in the future. Plus time to read, digest, learn, experiment, think, doodle, play, juxtapose. Plus the discipline to get your work started, completed, and continued.

I can't tell you specifically what book or journal you need to master your field of expertise. You're a big person now. If you won't even take this step by yourself, forget the rest of them and join the other 99% who already think you're odd for having wasted so much time toying with that whatyacallit, that niche marketing.

But I can offer a guide to what I've been saying in this chapter that will help get you started:

(1.) Write down the specific niche market need you want to meet and the broader fields related to that need. If you want to show metallurgists how to flange aluminum piping, that is the specific need. To explore that need fully you must begin your research in the fields of metallurgy, physics, chemistry, and engineering. That research will probably lead you into other fields as well.

(2.) Go to the library of a major university and investigate the feasibility and cost of a computer search for all desired information. To keep the cost reasonable and the results useful work closely with the librarian to identify precisely what you want and in which categories this information can be found. (Don't limit yourself to university libraries, however. Are there specialized or corporate libraries that are more appropriate? Private holdings?)

(3.) If a computer search is not done, or to supplement it, check the following sources in the library: the card catalog (including microfiche and microfilm listings), the stacks themselves to find books either unlisted or poorly titled, the current *Subject Index To Books In Print* (which will list books published in the United States in the past few years, with publishers' names and addresses), the current *Forthcoming Books in Print* (to see which books will be released in the coming six months, with a short description of each and from which publisher they can be purchased), any Library of Congress subject index listings that are available, the many academic indexes with their obscure journals from across the world, newspaper indexes, perhaps *Wilson's Vertical File Index* or the ERIC listings of academic papers, plus of course the bibliographies of those books or items found. Don't forget that most items are available through interlibrary loan even though the holding library may be thousands of miles away. (Check Alden Todd's *Finding Facts Fast* or a similar library use guide. Ask those blessed reference librarians to help you intensify your hunt; they usually love the challenge.)

(4.) Prepare an annotated bibliography compiled from each of the books that you check about other books about your subject or closely related subjects. List the author or editor, full title, publisher, date of publication, and where you can find the book for later consultation (if you know). Add to that anything you know or can deduce from a catalog listing about that book's contents as it relates to your topic.

(5.) Remember that libraries usually confine their search to articles and books. Ask the librarian how or where you can find other resources and directories/indexes: newsletters, audio and video tapes, speeches, seminars, a list of consultants, a roll of experts in the specific field — then explore each of these as fully as possible.

(6.) Talk to people who are knowledgeable about your specific need. Much of the best information isn't in print or in visual form. It reposes in the heads of practitioners eager to share it with anybody who asks. Ask.

(7.) Some of those information bearers, however, are short of time, suspicious, or anxious to economize on that sharing so they will want to know precisely why you want to know that data. A fair question that requires a prepared answer. They are usually most receptive to sharing if you are writing an article or book about the subject in which they will be cited. That presumes, however, that you are professional in your interviewing techniques, as a serious writer would be. There are several how-to guides about interviewing that can impart the needed know-how.

I particularly like Michael Schumacher's *The Writer's Complete Guide to Conducting Interviews.*

To get where we proposed you sell expertise about vitally needed information to specific markets. No expertise, no sale.

Chapter 8

Customizing Your Information

The second letter of the magic three in niche marketing, the "C" of TCE, stands for customization. It's what separates you from anybody else simply selling to the masses.

To be well on the way to a six-figure income in 18 months, if not there, the information you sell must fit a specific, chosen market like a tailored glove — a glove that that market very much wants and needs.

Returning to our example earlier, you don't just sell information about insurance to anybody. There's nothing particularly wrong with offering general knowledge that meets a broad need. Done right, it can help millions and earn in a like fashion. But usually it's the long, slow, uncertain route.

Customizing is the fast, sure path if it's done properly. So you find a market you want to serve first and match it to your area of expertise. You know insurance and you would like to deal with other professionals. You list the kinds of professionals; the top three on your list are dentists, anesthesiologists, and neurosurgeons.

You ask yourself, "What do they desperately need to know about insurance? What in your field will make their lives better, richer, less stressful, less encumbered so they can do what they like to do most and best?"

The response you imagine: the less they know or have to do with insurance, the better. No news is good news. Yet in the real world they must deal with insurance — and be covered by it. So you talk to some practitioners from the three fields. You ask them, given that insurance is a reality in their professional world, if they could solve just one problem, the biggest insurance headache they have, what would it be?

To a person they give you the same response: "How can I get rid of — or at least pay a lot less for — malpractice insurance?" A million-dollar question.

With the professionals on your list paying thousands of dollars annually on malpractice insurance, they would pay dearly to save dearly if you could show them how. So your question becomes, "How much could they actually lower their malpractice premiums given ideal conditions? And how can the average practitioner create those ideal conditions?"

Customization. Not insurance but malpractice insurance. Not why you should love having it and race to get more but their need or wish: how the premium can be reduced.

Customize more. Look again at the three markets on your list and pick one, then focus all of your attention on that group.

You check the SRDS mailing lists and find that while the three groups are equally accessible and able to afford your services there are far more dentists than anesthesiologists or neurosurgeons. And dentists are more likely to be directly involved with their insurance policies and premiums. So you select dentists.

You scour the written information regarding dental insurance policies, talk with colleagues who frequently write them, and contact insurance firms for specific particulars. The shocking news: almost all dentists can lower their malpractice premiums 50% if they do certain things! Back up the money truck! Now you have to get the information to them.

The next logical question would be how you would do that. What means would you use to convert the information into a huge benefit for them and a lifelong windfall for you? Let's look obliquely at that now and focus on customization in this chapter.

You have one very simple task at hand: make yourself a full-blown expert on lowering malpractice insurance premiums for dentists. That is what distinguishes you from insurance generalists or even the broad-market malpractice insurance specialists. That's why dentists will invite you to address their convention, will travel to attend your seminars, and will buy your book and perhaps your tapes.

Later, once you have proved yourself fully and accurately informed about lowering premiums for dental malpractice insurance and have shown that you can take this topic and make it easily comprehensible, doable, and a font of great savings, dentists will turn to you to solve other, critical dentally-related problems too. That bond of trust must be earned first, though. You must form-fit your initial information to one of the dentists' greatest needs. Your information must look, sound, and think dental.

Said in another way, if you decide to write a book about this topic you don't call it *How to Lower Your Malpractice Insurance Premiums 50%.*

If you do the dentist will think it's for the anesthesiologist who imagines it's for the neurosurgeon who suspects it's for the herbalist who is certain it's for the chiropractor. So nobody buys it.

The dentist buys it because the title says *Dentists: How to Lower Your Malpractice Insurance 50%.* The first word proclaims a special book to show dentists how to reduce their malpractice insurance premiums 50%, with the implication that there is a special need that dentists have, a special way they reduce those payments, and this book is written to show what that need is and how it's met. It's for dentists only.

Therefore the book must read like the kinds of books that dentists read. It must look like the books they buy. If they pick hardback books with more charts than photographs, 12-point sans serif type, and wide outside page margins (so they can take notes), that is what your book will look like. If dentists prefer polysyllabic jawbreaking words with Latin roots, get out the medical dictionary. You're not writing a book to change their reading habits or tastes. The book is written to be bought, then read, then applied. Of the three bought is your first objective.

More customization. If 80% of the dentists are males and the median age is 46, your book will represent that balance. In the photographs of dentists shown, roughly eight of ten will be males. Some will be new graduates and some long in the tooth, but most will gravitate toward 46. The same with dentists interviewed. The reader will feel comfortable with the mix.

Where appropriate it will be written with the same buzz words that dentists use with each other, the slang and jargon that binds colleagues together.

In short, once you have found a need you must draw the solution as close to the needy as possible, so they see you as a colleague struggling side-by-side with them in the common toil. Beyond offering a clear, honest solution to a real need, the book should be sewn with a thread so fine that their turning to you for help is as natural as turning to another dentist to solve a problem only they can understand. In life you remain an insurance

expert and book writer. The customization reduces the differences by highlighting the bond between what you have to say
and what they need to hear.

How do you do that? I said it before: becoming an expert
takes a lot of work. Begin reading the books that your readers
read, and the journals, trade papers, and newsletters. Try talking with them, rubbing elbows at conferences, asking questions,
getting into their minds and skins, watching them work and
play.

I've spoken of dentists and malpractice insurance here, but
my subject could have been a thousand other, desperately needed
topics for a hundred other professionals or niche elements and
the message would be precisely the same: you must adapt the
broader topic to the narrower market, trim and stretch it so it's a
genuine fit, and then add the special touches that convert an
everyday garment acceptable to most wearers into a truly spectacular raiment worth thrice its weight because of its obvious
singularity.

Let me say it another way, for the last time. You can (1) tell
men in their forties how to be good fathers or you can (2) tell men
in their forties specifically how to love their children so those
children will spend their lives as fully loving spouses, warm and
outgoing people, and the best possible models for their own
grandchildren. If you converted those into titles of books, which
of the two do you think would be the most bought?

Customization.

Chapter 9

Expanding Your Core Information
by Many Means

Not everybody wants to receive information the same way any more than everybody wants their milk hot, with melted butter. Some prefer it tooth-chattering cold, or fat-free, or even in a brandy alexander.

Many also want their information offered in various formats so they can choose. A book or a report would be fine to read on a lazy Sunday afternoon but an audiocassette would be better to hear while driving through the desert.

Which brings us the third letter of the magic three, the "E" of TCE, which stands for "expanded."

One way to expand core information is to offer the same basic message by several or all of the many means most familiar to writers, speakers, and entrepreneurs: articles, books, reports, newsletters, talks, speeches, seminars, audio and videocassettes, compact discs, CD-ROMs, and consultation. Let's discuss that in this chapter.

Another way to expand core information is to offer it, reconfigured, to many markets. That could be done by one means or many. A generic book called *How to Lower Your Malpractice Insurance Premiums 50%* could be framed, then researched and rewritten to the many professionals it would serve, adding each group's name before the title, as we've illustrated with dentists. Thus other versions might be *Lawyers: How to Lower Your Malpractice Insurance Premiums 50%* and *Therapists: How to Lower Your Malpractice Insurance Premiums 50%*. Or the basic information, say, for lawyers might also be expanded by as many of the means as are practical and profitable, such as newsletters, speeches, seminars, and consultation. Let's discuss that in Chapter 10.

Or the subject itself, once you have established your exper‑ tise in it, can be expanded from the core outward. That new information, then, can be offered by many means and/or to many new markets, reconfigured as needed. That will be the topic of Chapter 11.

Now, though, let's pose the concept of offering one basic message by many means, and go into the specifics about those means in Chapters 13 and 14.

The underlying premise here is straightforward: many mes‑ sages — much information — lend themselves to explanation and demonstration in different ways, and many receiving that infor‑ mation prefer or learn it better by different means.

We all know people who learn best by reading. Put some‑ thing in print, let them read it, and it's "captured" forever. We know people who stumble through the reading but remember every word ever said — content, order, and inflection. They are formidable in arguments! And we know people who grasp visu‑ als best, forming the rest of their learning around sight and sometimes integrated motion.

Is it a surprise, then, that people buy information that way too, if it is available? Or refuse to buy it if it's not?

Then too, the learning situation can dictate the choice of format. Driving through that desert we just mentioned makes the availability of information that might otherwise be preferred in writing a blessing if it's on audio tape.

Those are some reasons why consumers prefer choices about how they receive your information.

From your perspective there are two more, powerful reasons for giving the buyers choices: one, it means that your message will be more sought and better learned, and two, there will be many more buyers. Translate the second into far greater profits.

The point is that some buyers will buy your information one way, say as an article in a magazine, then will buy your book to learn more. They may attend a related seminar you offer in their town, and might then purchase a set of audio or even video tapes that again explain and expand that initial message. One means, one sale; many means, many sales.

Beyond wanting to learn the information another way, peo‑ ple often want to buy more good things from a source that in‑ spires them. They are moved, convinced, impressed, driven to action. So they turn to another format to find reinforcement, to share again.

Be ready to provide your information a second way, or more — if it is possible and economically sensible. Remember, what you offer must be good the first time out to move people to want to buy it again. And it must be just as good every other time out, to sustain their good faith in your message and integrity.

In other words, there must be no degradation in content or quality as it is shared by other means. The buyer is seeking the same high standard simply offered in a different way. The information can be expanded, new examples can be added; it can be seen from a different angle or a visually unique perspective, but the core information must be retained, undiluted, its prime force intact.

As mentioned earlier, common means by which information is shared by writers, speakers, and entrepreneurs are articles, books, reports, newsletters, talks, speeches, seminars, audio and video tapes, compact discs, CD-ROMs, and consulting. We will discuss each of these in detail later.

Now let's select some of them and use them to demonstrate how expanding your core information by many means makes sense and cents.

Let's create a new example too, to expand your view of the ways that the concepts in this book might be applied.

One of my favorite seminar examples is fifth grade teachers. We've all had one; for a short time I even was one. Unsung heroes in our early days — and an ideal niche market: bearing a common identity, on many accessible and relatively inexpensive mailing lists, more than eighty thousand in number, with the needs and the desire to meet them and with some cash they will spend to do so.

Usually the two fastest ways to make an impact on a niche market are through books or seminars. Teachers are readers so I will start here with a book. What kind of book, then, could I offer that at least 10% of the fifth grade teachers would gladly, even gleefully, buy? First thoughts:

> *How to Be the Best Fifth Grade Teacher in America*
> *The Twenty Best Fifth Grade Teachers in America*
> *The 15 Best/Most Exciting Fifth Grade Science Experiments for Nonscientific Teachers*
> *The 15 Best/Most Exciting Fifth Grade Social Science Projects Wherever You Teach*
> *Making Every Day a Dynamite Learning Experience in Fifth Grade*

What do these have in common? Each comes from a fifth grade teacher's top priority need or desire. How would I know that? I would have talked to six, a dozen, lots of fifth grade teachers to see precisely what they want and need to know, then packaged one of the most critical responses in a book that highlighted the book's benefit(s) in the title.

Equally important, every title zeros in on, talks directly to, mentions the niche buyer. Not "teachers" or "primary grades" or "grade school" but "fifth grade." The fifth grade teacher (or the primary school principal) buys the book specifically because it focuses on that one critical year in students' lives when their age hits double digits, some girls are experiencing the first signs of puberty, most boys are getting their first sports skills in sync, and most teachers are seeing the delightful emergence of wee, thinking adults.

Plus the book, if applied, results in better teachers, better and fuller use of their skills, new techniques and knowledge, better students. In short, a positive reason for filling out the order form, digging up or requisitioning the money to pay for it, finding an envelope and a stamp, getting the order mailed — and reading the book when it arrives! Enough reasons to overcome buyer inertia.

Let me use *The 15 Best/Most Exciting Fifth Grade Science Experiments for Nonscientific Teachers* as our "many means" example.

A book alone about this topic might in fact suffice: each experiment fully explained and illustrated with simple, easy-to-follow examples that the teacher can use in the classroom. The text would explain what the experiment shows, in terms that teachers can share with fifth grade students as it is being conducted. It would also explain the ramifications of that experiment: what else it shows, how the same result might be achieved another way, what would happen if you changed certain steps in the experiment. It might tell how this fits into the grander human life structure, how if one enjoys this experiment they could find similar scientific activities in high school, college, and in a job. And much more, all on the text page.

The book might also contain tear-out pages to duplicate for in-class distribution, or have overhead projections or slides as part of a book-plus package. Alas, our first venture into other means!

You might use one of the experiments for a magazine article directed to fifth grade teachers, noting in the text or in the biographical slug identifying you as the author that this experiment is but one from *The 15 Best/Most Exciting Fifth Grade Science Experiments for Nonscientific Teachers.*

You might offer a series of several or even all 15 of the experiments as articles, each with the same source tag. Why would the reader then buy the book? Some won't, but many would want that material on hand in bound form to use year after year. (They'd be prime candidates to buy *15 More of the Best/Most Exciting Fifth Grade Science Experiments for Nonscientific Teachers* though!) And many of those teachers, alerted to the existence of your exciting, easy-to-share material, would be interested in buying it by the other means about to be mentioned. (And some, teaching grades above or even below fifth, might adapt the experiments to their students' needs, expanding your buying market beyond the niche.)

You might offer the book plus a set of 15 reports, each of one of the experiments written at fifth grade level to be given to students at the proper time. Teachers would either buy the reports separately, an initial number would accompany the book when purchased, or they would buy the rights to reproduce the reports.

Newsletters are an excellent way to continue to serve a penetrated niche market. Once the teachers have identified themselves as buyers of fifth grade scientific information (when they buy the book), why not offer them a monthly newsletter, something like "Fifth Grade Science!", that not only includes a new experiment each issue, it's also packed with exciting scientific information broken into two segments, one for the teacher to integrate into classroom preparation, the other for student use, to be duplicated (perhaps to be shared with parents), passed around, posted on the bulletin board, or discussed by the new science club or cluster that is now possible with all this new fifth grade scientific information?

The topic can also be approached from the spoken perspective. By making *The 15 Best/Most Exciting Fifth Grade Science Experiments for Nonscientific Teachers* widely available you are indirectly advertising yourself as an expert about the teaching of fifth grade science, and perhaps of "fifth grade science" itself. Presuming the book is good, the more teachers who use it the greater your fame spreads and the firmer their perception of your expertise is rooted.

Experts have a reason to be booked for talks or speeches to those who would benefit from their expertise. If you offered seminars and invited fifth grade teachers to them from the general area, they would have a particular reason to attend.

How many teachers would eagerly budget for the inclusion of your video tape series, *The 15 Best/Most Exciting Fifth Grade Science Experiments for Nonscientific Teachers on Video*? Particularly after reading your book and deciding which experiment they would like to conduct in class and which they'd rather see done by you? So you might offer all 15 experiments as a series but each also available separately.

The financial implications of having the same core information available by many means is obvious. Yet it has a less evident multiplier effect. Those attending your seminar will often buy your book, subscribe to your newsletter, and may even purchase part or all of the video series. Those reading your book and noting the other ways additional information can be purchased on a back page order form may likewise indulge by other means. It was said earlier: more good things from the same trusted source.

Everybody wins if you can satisfy your niche's greatest needs, plus make available the learning or use format best directed to each buyer's wants.

That there may be many more buyers for that information is the topic of Chapter 10: Expanding Your Core Information to Many Markets.

Chapter 10

Expanding Your Core Information to Many Markets

If you are an expert about one subject to one specific niche market you can usually become, with a bit more work, an expert about that subject to many markets.

For example, if you are a writer of as-told-to books for professional basketball players you may need but a modest spurt of research and a change of hats to write similar books for professional baseball players, tennis stars, or even football coaches.

Seen from the perspective of a product, recall again the generic book *How to Lower Your Malpractice Insurance Premiums 50%* mentioned in the last chapter. That could be researched and specifically written to each of the many professionals afflicted by malpractice insurance. In addition to dentists, other versions might be *Lawyers: How to Lower Your Malpractice Insurance Premiums 50%* and *Therapists: How to Lower Your Malpractice Insurance Premiums 50%.*

The key point is that you are usually an expert about something first and how it applies to a particular group second. The core of that expertise is normally broad, deep, and basic; its application to a group is relative and specific.

While of course there is an interrelatedness, there is also a clear distinction between the core and its application. Generally the core is open-ended when it comes to learning. It is dynamic, ever-changing, and composed of so many parts one's expertise is never total. Yet learning how to apply the information is usually singular to the group applying it, and fully knowable, though new facets might develop and techniques might change over time.

Having said that, given one new wrinkle you might know all you need to know about applying it to another group. Change three or four steps and sometimes you can cover just about anybody using the basic information.

What you have then is one informational base, one core of expertise, packaged by how it is applied, like lower malpractice insurance premiums for dentists, lawyers, therapists, plus many others, like oculists, nurses, and nephrologists. One root, a bit more work, many markets. Quickly you are an expert to many more buyers.

We might break this interrelated dichotomy into three categories lest this discussion become too theoretical and term-laden. Let's define these categories by the core topic and call them the (1) single market niche topic, (2) multiple market niche topic, and (3) broad market niche topic.

The single market niche topic has been well discussed in earlier chapters. *Dentists: How to Lower Your Malpractice Insurance Premiums 50%* and *The 15 Best/Most Exciting Fifth Grade Science Experiments for Nonscientific Teachers* are examples, each directed to one market alone: respectively, dentists and fifth grade teachers.

That is where one starts — and sometimes finishes, by choice. It is where you initially hang your reputational hat. It is how you make your splash in that specific world — and get well paid, to afford future expansion. It is the expertise, the information and its application, that you are selling. Done right, it is why that topic and your name are synonymous in that niche field. You own that flag. You are that flag.

The concept, its application, and the market are the same whether they are sold by one means or many. It says: I know this well and will continue to know it better and better. Here is where I informationally and applicationally rule. My market for the very specific kind of information I have is dentists (fifth grade teachers, hockey players, CEO's). I also know precisely how they apply my information. And I'm dedicated to knowing every innovation, restructuring, and change in this field and its application.

For a relatively fast, then continual, six-figure reward and an 18-month toehold, this is how you start. Focus zealously on one topic for one niche market. Learn all there is to learn, let those in the market know you are there and the kind of help you can provide for the burning question(s) or critical need(s) they have, and spread your offerings out by the appropriate means. Sink roots while you learn and earn.

The multiple market niche topic is the theme of this chapter, expanding the single market niche topic. It says that once you have mastered the core information and know fully how it is applied to one field — and have presumably sold widely to that field, for the other kinds of learning experience that brings you — you are expanding that core to other, usually related fields.

The benefits of doing this are obvious. You can increase your income manifold while helping far more people, all while adding to your expertise for a fraction in the time, cost, and energy that it took you to obtain the original informational base.

If you are selling information by many means, it is also far less expensive to produce subsequent products. The second book is faster than the first; the sixth audiocassette uses the same tape deck and follows a now familiar path of preparation and production. And you are more accustomed to the promotional vehicles and processes. You're more likely to sell more and quicker; you are less likely to repeat the truly stupid mistakes that information-selling novices, like most novices, commit the first time out.

And by spreading your informational base into other markets you are less susceptible to the economic weaknesses in any one field. You might even stumble into a new pocket of prosperity!

You avoid another potential problem as well: boredom. One subject to one market can get old quick. One to many markets, less likely.

But there are three drawbacks to multiple market niching: one, there is the possibility that you will spread out too quickly, before you really learn the root information fully or well for any one field; two, that you will fail to keep up with the changes in your core field and thus lose that thoroughness that makes your expertise so valuable, or three, that you will fail to detect and master the unique areas of new learning required by each new field either in its broader informational base or in its application techniques.

How do you find those other markets where your information would be highly sought? In *Empire-Building by Writing and Speaking* I fully develop the concept of topic-spoking. Let's use it in this chapter in its simplest form.

Remember our book for teachers, *The 15 Best/Most Exciting Fifth Grade Science Experiments for Nonscientific Teachers*? Let's convert that from a book title into a description of the core topic, the expertise, that that book (and by extension you) sells: how to teach science to fifth grade students.

Now place that in the center of a circle of spokes that radiate from it. Let's use eight spokes, though it could be two, five, or 37.

Then ask yourself, to what other markets could you also offer that basic information, properly modified to meet their needs? Put those potential markets at the end of the spokes, one per.

If we hold with "science" as the teaching core, to whom else might we offer similar but modified information? Probably the teacher of any other grade that studied science. That might be as low as first grade and as high as ninth before science is customarily broken into specializations. Bingo! Our topic-spoking symbol would look like this:

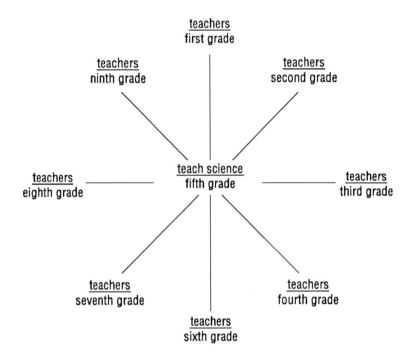

We've filled our spokes by just putting the different grade teachers at the end of each! That was easy! Let's go have pizza!

Slow down: we're not done yet. Why not think again about that word "science"? In high school science, students also study biology, physics, and chemistry. Would it be possible to create five super/exciting fifth grade physics experiments for nonscientific teachers? If so, to develop a physics learning track through-out the grade schools, why not the same for each of those other years too? (The teaching book then becomes *Fifteen Su-per/Exciting Physics Experiments for Grades 1-3 for Nonscien-tific Teachers*, with a second book for teachers of grades 4-6 and a third, of grades 7-9, at which point the physics textbook incorpo-rates and builds upon the lessons learned during those earlier grades.) Thus the core of this topic-spoking diagram says "teach physics," with the markets, the teachers to the respective grades, at the end of the spokes.

And if this can be done with physics, why not biology and chemistry, and if so why not five super/exciting experiments per year, with three more books for each topic?

But if the lower grade science program is going to be special-ized in this fashion, where or how do students learn the basics of science from which the disciplines come? Where do they learn the principles of nature and how natural law is observed, tested, and the interrelatedness of the experiments in biology, physics, and chemistry are comprehended?

Perhaps then, in addition to five super experiments in each of the three disciplines annually directed at each grade level, what is also needed is a book like *Ten Super Unifying General Science Experiments for Fifth Grade Nonscientific Teachers*, one for teachers of each year that the program covers. This book would be the teacher's guide to bringing a fuller understanding of science in the universal sense as well as integrating the other discipline-based experiments into a comprehensive science pro-gram for each academic year.

Or all 25 experiments — 10 general and 15 by the disci-plines — could be combined into a book, one for each of the first nine graded academic years, each including a teacher's integrat-ing guide.

You've taken a huge leap from one book and one grade to many books and a full two-school science curriculum! Beware: a bit of uncontrolled paper thought, some wild spoke spinning, a few reckless "what if's?...," and you can suddenly find yourself a new American scientific mastermind! On paper.

But who will pay any attention to you and your ideas unless you are indeed a master of a topic at some point, with displayed expertise, a successful track record, and teaching/learning re-sults that command respect? To change the niche world you can plot fast but you usually move slowly because you must prove yourself to every new niche element. From a single market niche topic and mastery to a multiple market niche topic, all in due time, each move oiled by excellence.

As long as we are using topic-spoking to show how you might expand your niche marketing, why not practice it once again, with a familiar example?

Let's return to our original topic-spoking diagram with "teach science/fifth grade," plus, below it, "15-experiment book" in the center and the spokes projecting. Restricting yourself solely to science and fifth grade, you ask by what other means, in addition to the book *The 15 Best/Most Exciting Fifth Grade Science Experiments for Nonscientific Teachers*, might you share the book's system and information with fifth grade teachers? If you write down the means already discussed in this book at the end of each spoke, your new diagram would look this way:

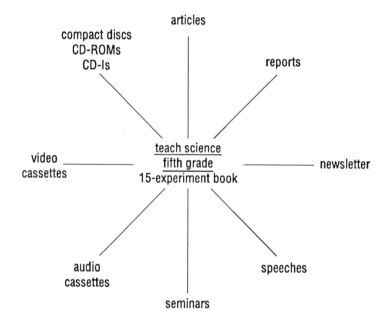

The next step is to analyze how each of the means might be used to bring more information about the book — its existence, contents, or message — to the fifth grade teachers and/or their students. If the means are inappropriate you simply remove that spoke.

Selecting "seminars" as an example, you could offer seminars (or workshops) to fifth grade teachers about the ways they could perform the 15 experiments and how these fit into the greater science learning world for children at that age. Or you could go to the fifth grade classroom itself and speak — or to an assembly of all the fifth grade students from that school or all of the schools in town. You could offer your seminar to college students training to teach primary school. You could offer it to retirees who will tour the schools conducting these experiments for fifth grade classes. Or to superintendents to show them how exciting science can be in the fifth grade and why they need your concept and book in their system.

And of course if this can be done with fifth grade teachers about science, all of the expanded forms above — the disciplines or unifying science experiments as well as teachers at each of the other grade levels — lend themselves to similar presentation by seminars.

After asking these questions about seminars, do the same for each of the other means. Then ask yourself how you might combine two or three means to add effectiveness, depth, and — yes, profits.

I know, just thinking about the potential is exhausting. This niche marketing isn't for the faint of heart. You see why the other 99% are gleefully doing something else? You're in that special 1%. World changers. Keep reading....

Let me suggest another multiple market niche topic that almost anybody can do in almost any field of endeavor: the "state of the art in ...."

Meat packers, brain surgeons, plumbers, librarians, hardly a soul doesn't bristle with curiosity about how other people do what they do here and abroad. Particularly if they do it more easily, better, faster, or use new gadgetry. They also want to know how things will be in a year, two years, and five years. (A bit of the past also helps to see how far they have come since...)

This kind of information is avidly sought for articles, books, keynote speeches at conventions, newsletters, and consultation. CEO's and planning honchos need to know it. And it's fairly easy to get. Read, ask, read, compare, read, and look where experimentation, study, and development are taking place. Much of it is common sense, projection, and observation, plus a fair dose of asking that mutinous question, "what if...?"

Once you get close to the state-of-the-art in your chosen field, it doesn't take a quantum leap to ferret out other states-of-the-art for related markets.

Let's close this chapter by discussing the broad market niche topic, which sounds like a contradiction in terms.

In essence, you take a subject that would interest many people and you customize it to that element of society to whom you are speaking. You expand this to many markets simply by finding a new audience and customizing it again.

An example works best here, one close to my heart since it is a speech I offer widely called "Five Ways You Can Change the World." The topic is broad but if the listeners are counterfolk in a fast food chain the way they can change the world differs dramatically from an audience composed of cloistered monks.

If this is your topic, your responsibility as we have defined it in this book is to have a full comprehension of how people can in fact change the world, then evaluate your listeners — or readers, viewers, or recipients of your information by whatever means — and convert your knowledge to their needs and capacities of application. It would be unkind to suggest that cloistered monks can change the world by tap-dancing in music halls. And cruel to suggest to fast food salesfolk that they ignore their customers and chant.

As in other areas, here you are an expert about the topic first, as much as one can be, and how it applies to a particular group second. But the selection of ways and the application is what makes this form of niche marketing rather upside down since almost any eager audience will do. You specialize it by selecting the ways that particular audience can change the world.

In Chapter 11 let's quickly discuss a concept we have already lightly touched: how one expands the core information itself.

Chapter 11

Expanding the Core Information Itself

Perhaps the most obvious way to move out from, or expand, a core topic is to look inward: to further develop component or essential aspects of the topic itself. That can then be offered by many means and/or to many new markets, reconfigured as needed.

In Chapter 9, using fifth grade teaching as the pivotal activity, we asked how we could create the best science experiments for students at that level. We then saw how we could stretch our effectiveness, breadth, and profits further by using additional means to explain that science — articles, reports, seminars, videocassettes, and more.

In the last chapter we saw how we could expand that same concept to many markets, in this case by adapting the fifth grade science teaching format to teachers at all primary and middle school grades, from first to ninth. And how we could find "state-of-the-art" markets just about anywhere we had the "art."

In a way what is being suggested here cannot help but happen any time you expand the sharing of your core information by other means or to other markets.

For example, when you added courses in physics and chemistry to your basic fifth grade science classes, your core information was also expanded. As it was when you offered those courses to grades other than fifth.

Yet here you dig in one mine only. New veins but the same pit.

Let's say that in this case your primary concern is less science than fifth grade. You have created a system or approach that has at its core the development of the very best fifth grade teachers possible — and you've chosen science as the initial subject for demonstration.

Continuing to use our new plotting technique, topic-spoking, put "fifth grade/science" in the center. Then ask, "To what other subjects might I apply my system at the fifth grade level?" Write the other subjects that fifth graders are taught, or could be, at the end of the spokes. Then analyze each of those to see if you can or want to expand your expertise into it.

If the spokes include, say, English, mathematics, social science, geography, health, physical education, music, and art, you might take any of them, see if you could create the qualitative equivalent to *The 15 Best/Most Exciting Fifth Grade Science Experiments for Nonscientific Teachers* in that field, and consider, if you wish, adding that expertise to your widening base.

Your core subject is fifth grade teaching. That's what you know best. When others hear that topic, your name comes to mind — or should. You know where fifth grade students are intellectually and emotionally. You know what they have (or should have) learned by fifth grade, what they want and need to know during that year, and the best ways to bring that knowledge to them. You test, strengthen, and display your expertise by teaching fifth grade science; now you want to apply your deeper understanding of the greater concept of "fifth grade teaching" to other areas beyond science.

It's one mine, one excavation. Your wealth is teaching at the fifth grade level. The deeper you dig the more gems you find, and share: different techniques, different topics, different combinations.

Then you can expand your teaching efficacy at that level by using many means. You take the discipline(s) or subject(s) to be taught by your fifth grade method and topic-spoke it or them by the means. One of those disciplines might be English, so in the center of the diagram you would write "fifth grade English." Some of the means at the end of the spokes might be books, software, or reports.

The result? How might you use what you know about teaching English to fifth graders by using those means? Perhaps a book called *Ten Sensational Writing/Reading Projects for Fifth Grade English*, an interactive computer program that helps students create their own short story structure, or a how-to report about writing haiku poetry.

In other words, before hunting for other means or markets you might simply stay at home, dig more deeply into the core subject itself, and see how many of its components could be developed into new niche marketing concepts. The strength of this approach roars: rather than moving into a new territory to create a new font of expertise, you are instead becoming even more expert on something you know well, presumably like and care about, and where you are already a recognized authority.

"Words are the only things that last forever."

William Hazlitt (1778-1830)

"What another has done as well as you, do not do it. What another would have said as well as you, do not say it; written as well, do not write it. Be faithful to that which exists nowhere but in yourself — and thus make yourself indispensable."

André Gide (1869-1951)

Chapter 12

Niche Marketing: Determining the Purpose and Defining the Means and Markets

To make yourself indispensable, slightly immortal, and life-long rich it's not enough just to have critical information that others would gladly pay to know, you have to put that information into some intelligible and exchangeable format, then exchange it. Usually sell it.

That format generally involves the written word on paper or disk for writers or in some spoken mode, directly or on tape or compact disc, for speakers. Some, ambitious and well gifted, will sell information both written and spoken. So will most entrepreneurs.

Your Purpose in Niche Marketing

But before honing in on the ways that would put you the golden trail, you must first determine what you expect to get in return for exchanging your own special, marketable knowledge.

By knowing what kinds of rewards you want, and when, you can then select the means and the kind and number of markets required to help you earn those rewards — assuming they can be earned at all.

If you expect to earn one million dollars a day from writing articles, you are chewing something illegal. Can't be done. Conversely, if you want to speak to throngs and earn $37 a week, that's about as hard. If you are any good at all only a true Scrooge would pay you that little, and if you're not worth $37 a week you won't earn anything at all!

In Chapter 4 we spoke of a three-pronged life-planning approach. The first asks the kind of life you want to lead on this earth. Let's focus on the second and third prongs and rely on you to keep those consistent with that desired kind of life.

The second asks where you want to be by at least eight criteria in five years, and the third prong, where you want to be in between, using one-year anniversaries to gauge your progress. Here we will use but one criterion — income — and again let you bring the others — job, position, equity, expenses, marital status, children, reputation, other assets — into line with your life goals.

New venturists, I have found, usually fall into one of two categories: those who want it all instantly at almost any cost and those who are already burdened, working hard, have little margin for risk, and expect to take a much longer period of time.

Let's call the first "Lightning Lee" and the second "Cruising Kim."

Lightning Lee has, say, an income goal of $100,000 the first year, $250,000 the second, $450,000 the third, $700,000 the fourth, and seven figures every year thereafter.

Cruising Kim, no less ambitious but far less free to pursue the niche market at the outset, would be elated to earn $15,000 more in 12 months and $25,000 in 24. Then Kim could ease into niche marketing full-time and would expect $65,000 the third year, $125,000 the fourth anniversary, and $200,000 the fifth.

Defining the Means and Markets

This tells us one thing immediately: Lee needs to serve more markets or sell more information, probably by more means and far faster, than Kim. And that helps us evaluate the tools at their disposal from at least that measure: those that will bring the greatest and quickest rewards are where Lee must head. Kim has more time to develop and strengthen the selling base, but in the third year Kim too must almost certainly switch to income-intensive means and probably more markets.

Yet both share one thing in common: from the beginning they must evaluate the three ways they can multiply income from one information core. Can they expand the core itself to offer more, related information? Can they offer what they know to more markets? Can they do it by more than one means? Or can they create and sell more by some combination of these three basic approaches? (Or can they think of another effective approach?)

This book addresses itself to the means most commonly used by writers, speakers, and entrepreneurs — and would address the other two more fully were that possible, that is, were they not so intimately related to the niche topic itself, of which there could be thousands.

Selecting the most appropriate means by which your subject might best be niche marketed requires some research. You must know:

(1) What other information exists, directly like yours or similar, and whether it is accessible to your market.

(2) By what means is it available?

(3) How is it packaged?

(4) What are its informational limits?

(5) How much does it cost?

(6) How widely is it bought?

(7) Can it be improved in content, quality, appearance, cost, promotion, delivery, or other ways?

(8) How much demand exists in your market for more of that information, as is or improved?

Further, you should have that information, as it is sold, at hand. If at all possible, buy anything you can get and study it thoroughly.

You also need a sense of what information like yours is likely to become available to your market in the future, when, by what means, and roughly what it will cover and cost.

Then topic-spoke that core subject by all of the means by which that information is now being bought, or might be in the future, by your market.

Next, if it's presently being bought, evaluate those means by the answers to the questions above. And if it's not, would people buy it by other means if it were available? How would they hear about it by those means? Where would they buy it? Those are the questions to ask of every conceivable means as it relates to your market.

That's where knowledgeable friends can be extremely helpful: to brainstorm, to ask the "what if's...?" to help provide needed answers and perhaps suggest a unique angle or way to serve your market ahead of slower competition.

Take the means-related information you gather and the ideas you generate and put the means most appropriate to providing your special knowledge to your niche market in some priority order. That order will correspond directly to your purpose. If generating income is paramount, that becomes the top priority. Other criteria vying for pre-eminence are the positioning value of the first information sold, the mode of purchase most sought by buyers, the availability of selling venues for that means, the cost of using that means to market, and sometimes the logical development of the information itself.

Most of those are readily understandable without further explanation. But let me elaborate on two that might be less evident.

The positioning value of the first information sold is very important. If you want to quickly establish your niche field as yours alone, to get quickly and firmly rooted as "the" expert in the area before others leap onto the bandwagon, you want to pick a means that is marketed widely and fully to all in your market. Usually a book or seminar does this best, though a well placed article first can set the pace and tone, heralding your name before it's seen again, often on a flyer sent by mail. Conversely, creeping into a field with marginal products that treat some side element of your topic has little positioning value and may motivate others who are more aggressive to rush in to meet the core niche need.

Another priority might not be obvious, that of the logical development of the information itself. An example might show this best. You want to become the catcher's catcher in baseball, the teacher of all that catchers ever need to know. You want to create and sell a definitive how-to program that would begin with new, current catchers or those fresh to baseball and considering moving behind the plate. You plan to do this through a video series on the fundamentals, supported by strategically placed articles in sports magazines read by youngsters and coaches, a series of booklets, and a book.

But if you start with throwing techniques used by college catchers designed to snare professional scouts' attention, you are starting your race from the finish line! Your initial market wants and needs the fundamentals, the basics, the core elements. Once they have become steady patrons, fans of your first-rate developmental program, they will clamor for the refinements. First you must get them involved where their interest is greatest, then help them progress to higher levels by maintaining the same top quality offerings in concert with their growing capacities.

So here you topic-spoke the means and prioritize them to match your niche marketing purpose. To do that you need some particulars about how the means meet the niche marketing demands. So let's discuss that for the next two chapters, then attempt to tie it all together in Chapter 16.

"It is in spending oneself that one becomes rich."

Sarah Bernhardt (1844-1923)

Chapter 13

Niche Marketing by Writing

The question is how well the various means of sharing information work for niche marketing.

The answer(s) for each of the information dissemination means are, of course, relative rather than absolute since each means must be considered many ways: alone, jointly with another means, and in combination with many means. And what works uncommonly well with one topic or to one market might be a whopping dud with another.

There is another set of factors: how much of or how often the means are used, the context in which they are used, and how well they are used. An article run once in a magazine never read by your buying market will be decidedly less effective than a key column run monthly in the most sought publication. Likewise, a dumb book or an error-ridden report will sell some early copies but will prove, and be reinforced by reviews and word of mouth, that the reader should consciously avoid anything else you produce in that field.

Because of the variables we could throw our hands in the air and wish you good luck or we could set up a guideline to apply to all of the written and spoken means discussed in this and the next chapter, so that one means could be roughly compared to another when you establish your niche marketing plan. The guideline follows.

Articles

What is the best way to use articles for niche marketing?

Articles are most effective when they appear in publications most read and respected by your niche buyers. By extension, articles appearing in poorly produced magazines or newspapers — shoddy appearance, low quality thinking, poor writing or editing, unsubstantiated conclusions, too much variance in the article's composition or presentation from the norm — may be worse than nothing at all. Still, in general a solid article in a reputable publication is positive and can display your expertise widely.

Also, if the niche topic has political overtones, being at the far ends of the political spectrum can either augment or reduce your topic's acceptance by the reader. An essay bubbling with liberal rhetoric, for example, won't solicit subscriptions from readers much to the right.

But let's assume for these pages that you first review all of the potential publications where your topic would be appropriate and you delete those not serving your purposes. The rest you will want to list in priority order by how effectively they will help you niche market. Put them into two lists: magazines and newspapers.

Magazines

You would begin the magazine list by querying the editor of the top magazine, showing in a well written one-page letter what you want to write about, why readers would be interested, why you are qualified to write the article, and anything more needed to acquaint the editor with the topic. The query letter should sell your idea and you as the person to write it by the way it is written.

The query should also be written in the style of the article you would write should you receive a positive reply. That is, if you wish to write a humorous piece, the letters should be humorous to the same degree. If it's to be fact-packed and written in racehorse style, so should read the query. Show you can do it later by doing it in the letter.

Querying is fully explained, with 20 samples, in my recent book, *Writer's Guide to Query Letters and Cover Letters*.

If you have three different articles you want to write and seven magazines where it is in your best interests to appear, there are several ways to begin. You can start with the top magazine, the first on your list, and query it about the best topic of the three. If that editor says no, you query the next, and so on until your idea has been accepted or you have exhausted all seven possibilities. Then you start with the second best topic....

Or you could query the top magazine about the best idea, the second magazine about the second idea, and the third, the third. If any say yes, bingo. That article appears and stops there. But if they say no, you keep them going downward, always returning after a rejection to the best magazine still unqueried. If the top magazine rejects the top idea and the second, the second best, try the second idea with the top market. (They don't know it's your second choice. Don't tell them either, just query with full vigor.) The rule of thumb, assuming that all publications are national in scope, is never to compete with yourself; never have more than one query before an editor at one time. And always send a stamped, self-addressed envelope (SASE) for a reply.

There are three kinds of replies, with variations, that you can expect. No reply, no, or yes.

Wait two months before worrying about no reply. Then copy your query (always keep a copy of the original) and attach a note to it that makes three points: (1) the query attached to your note was sent on ___ date, (2) perhaps it got lost in the mail, and (3) is the subject still as exciting now for the editor's readers as it was then? A gentle prodding. Mail it. If you don't hear in another 30 days the editor isn't interested or the magazine has folded, probably the latter. Rewrite the query and send it to the editor of the next magazine on your list.

If the reply is no, thank God you didn't write the article for that deadhead editor! Don't brood. Study the next magazine, write a good query to that editor, and see what happens. You will gather far more rejections than acceptances however good or desperate you are. But look hard at each rejected query before reworking it. Does it grab your attention? Is it exciting? Does it make an editor want to call you immediately? If not, pump some life into it before you subject another editor to it! Another rejection? You must be getting closer to success: redo it and send it to the third editor. An idea that good somebody has to buy!

You're saying to yourself, "Why don't I just make seven copies and send one each to all seven editors at once?" The reason is painfully simple: most editors want to have material appear on their pages first, therefore they want to buy first rights. There is only one first rights. If you get two or three editors champing at the bit, you're in big trouble because you must say no to somebody — a somebody who won't buy from you in the future. So do as professionals do: query one at a time, in order of your preference.

And if an editor says yes? What a bright person, and what good taste! The editor will tell you when the material is needed — or you should assume it must be there within three weeks. (Travel writing has different demands here so I refer you to my latest book, *The Travel Writer's Guide*, for those deviations as well as the full process.)

Your words in print should be a big niche marketing plus — if your article shows you to be bright, well informed, and a possessor of information readers need. You usually do that by giving the editor precisely what you promised in the query letter written to the level of other articles on those pages. Every time your niche market reads something you have written, it judges you. So this and all articles must be carefully crafted to show you as scrupulously honest, clear, eager to help, and sharing some element of your specialty in such a way that each reader — a potential buyer — is left knowing that you know much more than the space limitations permitted and wondering how to learn more from you in the future.

There are many books in public libraries that will show you how to prepare manuscripts for submission. My *How to Sell More Than 75% of Your Freelance Writing* also does that, in addition to offering a hundred more pages about selling, and reselling, magazine and newspaper articles.

Newspapers

Newspapers buy less outside copy than magazines. You or your topic are more likely to be written about by a journalist, over which you have little control in terms of what is said, than to have the words written for print by you.

But newspapers do buy "special" pieces, usually for the op-ed, travel, food, or family pages — or unique features. Uniqueness and/or timeliness are almost always the criteria for consideration: what can you tell the reader of that newspaper that they can't get elsewhere or don't know? Particularly, what's new (hence newspaper), what's about to break, what's different and about to be revealed?

Most newspaper editors don't like to be queried but would rather see the article in final form. Send it double-spaced with a cover note or letter attached that explains in the opening paragraph or two what the article is about, why you wrote it, and why readers would care. Include a paragraph indicating the photos you can provide (probably in black and white), if you can and they are interested. Include an SASE.

Again, the *Writer's Guide to Query and Cover Letters* as well as *How to Sell More Than 75% of Your Freelance Writing* describe the newspaper process fully, with examples.

Can you query first? Of course, but newspaper editors are often too harried to respond. If the newspaper is local and you know the particular editor's name, you could call and ask if they'd be receptive to an article about that topic. If it's distant, you can check the name and number in the current *Working Press of the Nation* in your local library.

Most magazines are national in distribution so you must query and sell first rights to them one at a time. That is so for the "national" newspapers as well such as the *New York Times*, *Wall Street Journal*, *U.S.A. Today*, and the *Christian Science Monitor*.

But other newspapers will almost always accept copy as long as it's not been sold to another newspaper or magazine within their 100-mile distribution range. Thus you can send the same completed manuscript simultaneously to as many newspapers that meet that geographic stipulation as you wish. You needn't tell them it is simultaneously submitted unless they ask; they will assume you are doing as indicated.

One more peculiarity regarding newspapers. They often buy from syndicates, which sell columns, series, and sometimes single articles to many clients. You have no control over the targeting other than selecting a syndicate that sells to the kinds of newspapers in which you want your material to appear. But it is one way to be seen widely in print by your niche market with a minimum of mailing yourself. The current *Writer's Market* provides 50+ listings. You can also consult the *Editor & Publisher Syndicate Directory* in your library.

Or you can mini-syndicate it yourself, which is what you are doing by sending the same piece simultaneously to newspapers outside each other's primary distribution range.

In most other ways magazines and newspapers are similar, except two. Newspapers work on a much faster deadline, so three weeks often becomes three days (or even three hours) for a newspaper. And the writing style is generally more compact in newspapers: write well but even more tightly.

A final thought for both magazines and newspapers, in case it's not obvious. Get a byline! That means "by (your name)" under the title. Why do all this work if readers don't link you to the vital information they are reading? Sometimes editors will add biographical information about you, called a "bio slug." Write your own, one to three sentences, the shorter the better. Include what your niche market needs to know, the most important first. If you wrote an article about a new process for preparing personalized face cream, don't toot your soccer prowess or that you have nine daughters. You are selling a new process to a particular market. Describe yourself as an expert, creator, developer — whatever honestly distinguishes you — then build from that. Forget the editorial superlatives: "the greatest," "*número uno*,"... But do include your address and phone number. Editors rarely use them but why not try?

How profitable are articles in magazines and newspapers?

In themselves not very profitable, if at all. But they can lead to a good return.

Magazines pay anywhere from nothing, or a few free copies of the issue, to many thousands of dollars. Most pay from $150 750 per article, plus $15-100 per b/w photo or color slide. The current *Writer's Market* provides specific amounts for most magazines. The check is sent either when the piece is bought or, less commonly, when it is published.

Newspapers vary widely, most paying $50-350 on publication, usually on the lower side of that range, plus $15-50 per b/w photo. Some don't pay at all, figuring that the worldwide celebrity resulting from having your words on page 12, section D, is worth more than you would want or could handle.

How can you increase the worth of your article beyond that modest payment?

The best way is to write an article so stunning, so clear, so compelling that every reader in your niche market would cut it out, reread it repeatedly, and call several friends to discuss your prose and message. That would naturally lead them and their now enlightened friends to contact you to buy anything you are selling.

A snip of exaggeration but articles can come close to that. First, find in your pool of information something that all readers would be interested in knowing and that your niche folk probably don't know either. Second, if your writing is mediocre, get the piece sharpened up. Third, work in a reference to your most appropriate or accessible product. And fourth, ask the editor to include your address or phone in the bio slug "so you can directly field the calls that will come and it won't burden the editor or the newspaper having to refer them." Let's discuss each of these separately.

The information you write about is critical. It should be central or closely related to your core area of expertise so the reader clearly makes that association. It must be something your niche market needs to know: a clarification, expansion of its present knowledge, something new or unique, or a blending of it with other information in a valuable new way. And it must be of interest to the broader public also reading the publication.

How you write about it is important too. Articles are composed of facts, quotes, and anecdotes — usually plenty of the first deftly intermingled with a few anecdotes (if appropriate; examples can often be added or substituted) and two to four key quotes. The resulting composition must make sense, say something fresh or freshly presented, do so smoothly in proper English, and flow from point to point with ease. You will be judged on your articulation: on how well and clearly you join the parts together.

The facts must be accurate. If unclear, they must be explained. If controversial, at least an overview of the argument must be offered, plus where those fit into that argument. If crucial, their source is important. Fleshing the facts out with at least a minimum of adjectives and adverbs is appreciated too.

Most of the telling facts come directly from quotations. Contact the most knowledgeable people in the field and ask them the key questions your article addresses. That and other printed sources will be the origin of most or all of your quotes.

One problem here is that you too are either a leading personality in your field or aspiring to be. Yet you can't quote yourself. But you can cite your own research. Or you can have a friend write the article and quote you at length, plus others. Or you can write the article, do the same, and have it marketed by your friend under his or her name. You lose the credit of authorship but you gain prominence as an expert. (If this is later discovered, though, it can tarnish your reputation.)

Why would you write an article if you can't feature yourself, since that would surely be a niche marketing plus? In part because by artfully pulling all of the facts and points together in print you elevate yourself, in many minds, to a higher plateau, to that of an expert readily adept at dealing and explaining all facets of the topic.

If your writing is mediocre, get the piece sharpened up. If it doesn't do what an expert should — show full grasp, read clearly, make a point, and all the rest just said — seek help to make this article your best possible show card.

For a modest fee, probably $25-100, find a rewriter who will take the written article and rework it into fit publishing form. That assumes you have everything researched and written. If rewriters must do more than write, fees quickly escalate.

Where do you find rewriters, usually called editorial assistants? Newspaper writers moonlight this way. So do other professional writers, English or composition teachers, most folks in journalism or advertising, often librarians. The *Yellow Pages* run advertisements for these services under "writing," as does the *Writer's Digest, The Writer,* and the *Literary Market Place.*

Why bother? Because you're posing as an expert in your niche field. Yet if you read something by an "expert" that bumbled along or was poorly organized and written or simply didn't show much competence because the person, while bright, had little facility with words, would you go to them for more expensive advice about a bigger niche problem? Hardly.

Third, work in a reference to your most appropriate or accessible product. Often this can't be done — or you don't have a product yet. But a readily acceptable way is to include your item(s), among others, in a general list in one place in the article (often at the bottom) or to refer to each when you discuss the related topic. Another way is to cite your product as the source at the bottom or end of the data listing.

You can either refer to your material precisely as you do all other references, you as the author by your full name, or you can simply say "my book" and then give the title. If you include an address and perhaps the price after the reference so the reader can order it, do the same to all currently available references. Mention of a second item by you or others is usually followed by the publisher's name only, if it is the same house. It's an excellent idea to list the address and price — although many editors will edit it out — since, if it survives, it leads your niche market directly to you. (Yes, it leads them to others too, but you wrote the article and their response, if any, is heavily weighted, however objectively done, in your favor.)

And fourth, ask the editor to include your address and/or phone number in the bio slug. Some editors will gladly do this, and even let you add in the key product(s) you offer plus their price(s) — list each postpaid and tax included. Some will include it in lieu of paying you, thinking that the response business generated through that full reference will more than compensate you for appearing on their pages. Often they are right. But most will limit you to a byline and sometimes a line or two more, without further references whatsoever.

There's one more technique you might consider if the editor responds negatively to promoting your products through a bio slug. Offer readers some additional free information about the topic discussed: "Five ways to...," "Three examples of...," "An illustrated diagram of..." These are usually a page or two in length. When you send the free item you also include all of your sales promotional material, plus you garner a name for the new mailing list you are building from any person or company requesting information or products. Of course to send the reader the information you must include your address in the bio slug! And for them to request the item by phone you must include your phone number! Everybody wins. (You can even ask the respondent to send a stamped, self-addressed envelope to offset postage, though that will limit your responses.)

One thing is certain, if you don't send in your biographical information and ask for a full reference listing, or suggest offering some free mailback, every reader will be deprived of valuable information about you and your products or services!

How much does it cost to use articles as a niche selling means?

Very little, other than the time spent gathering information and positioning your thoughts and words in the right order. Add a trip to the library to list the publications, editors, and addresses; some time at a word processor or typewriter; a mailing envelope and an SASE; the stamps, and putting the missive in the mail box.

If the first query or submission doesn't sell, more typing, envelopes, and stamps until one does.

Lately editors of perhaps 50% of the magazines and 40% of the newspapers have been requesting the material, once it has been accepted, on disk or by modem, if it's available that way. (We send it on a 5 1/4" floppy in three formats on the same disk: IBM/Sprint, Microsoft Word, and ASCII. Just ASCII is enough.) Not having the copy in computerized form doesn't kill a sale, however.

The anxiety of waiting is the heaviest toll.

Are articles a good "lead" means for niche marketing?

They can be in terms of displaying your expertise quickly and effectively and making your presence known to many in your market but they are only profitable when they lead the reader to buy your follow-up products or services. More on the latter in a moment.

To make that initial impact you must be in the key publications your market reads — or somehow reach celebrity status through other media, then tie your expertise in your niche field to that. Getting in the key publications you can control, so let's focus there.

If you don't know what your market reads, and which are their top publication choices, ask them. Or, if your market has an association or union, see if that information is available.

Then put those publications in readership order and focus on a "hot" issue related to your expertise. Query the editors in that order, and when you get a "go-ahead," write a first-rate article that clearly displays, by its structure and content, that you know the material and have a solution to the problem or an answer to a need.

Follow this spearhead article with others, always querying or submitting from the most read publication down. The more often those in the market see you as the information-bearer, the quicker they recognize you as the authority.

How are articles best integrated with other means?

Articles show that you know a subject well. They can also suggest that you are the person for follow-up information or services, particularly if the editor permits reference to your products and/or includes your address and phone/FAX either in the text or in your bio slug.

If you've written a book and the article is at all related to the book, you will want to refer to it: "excerpted from (the book title), published by (name) (copyright date in parentheses), (address where it can be purchased — the publisher or, preferably, you — and phone/FAX optional), cost postpaid ($__.__)." If it isn't excerpted from the text, just start with the word "from." For example,

"from *Self-Publishing to Tightly-Targeted Markets,* published by Communication Unlimited (1989), P.O. Box 6405, Santa Maria, CA (805) 937-8711, cost postpaid $16.45.

You could do the same with any other product from which the information derives, such as an audio or video tape, report, newsletter, or seminar. If the information is essentially the same in several means you could either select the means most likely sought by the reader for purchase or, if they have the same title, you might say, "from the book and videocassette," then list the title and the other data above, adding both prices at the end, following each with the means in parentheses.

Articles needn't be the lead item. Rather, as you prepare a tape script, a book, or a speech — any means — you can reassemble that information, query about the topic, and if the publication is interested, sell it as an article (or even as a series of articles) while the other means take form. That provides the expertise display you want, tells of the coming product from which it is extracted or excerpted, and earns a bit of money to invest in the new product. Or the reverse, wait until you have all of the material in final form, sell the product, and then sell excerpts from it.

Articles can also be used widely to promote you and your expertise once they are in print. The editor will send you a copy or two of the issue. Cut out the article, paste it up in running text fashion on the front and back of a page or two, and make many clear copies. Send these copies to anybody interested in you as a speaker, writer, or who simply wants to know about you. They are particularly impressive this way — if the article itself is good and displays you to your best advantage.

Any final thoughts about articles as niche marketing tools?

The previous sentence says, again, why you would even consider writing articles: they must focus fast and hard on you as knowledgeable, articulate, and organized, an expert on a subject of top interest to your niche buying market. Anything less and almost any other means would work better.

Chapter 13B

Books

What is the best way to use books for niche marketing?

Writing and publishing a book may be the most effective and substantial way to prove that you have something important to say, you know something that you think those in your niche market should know, its topic merits a full presentation (generally from one to several hundred pages of copy, plus artwork), and you are offering the material in a format that invites detailed analysis and review.

After all, a book is about as permanent a means as information disseminators can find, short of concrete or bronze. It can be read once or repeatedly, the words and the thoughts it expresses are frozen in place, the data can't change on the page, and even the stylistic innuendos and the choice of type and leading can be analyzed again and again.

It also says that you are intentionally entering the top echelon of idea creators or information molders in your niche field. Books don't casually happen. They require too much work, thought, and craft to be easily dismissed. A book puts you in the big leagues.

Alas, a bad book creates a major league bad impression. But a good book firmly plants you among the leaders. How firmly depends upon what you say, how you say it, what you use to support your message, what the book looks like, and how widely it is distributed and read.

For major impact the best way to use a book is to launch it hard, put full attention and funds into its promotion and distribution, get it read and reviewed as widely and quickly as possible, and follow it up with more of you, your products, and other books.

Done right, a book can be the best possible empire-building engine, with the other means dutifully following behind and multiplying its profit and effectiveness. The engine leads, toots, roars, cuts through the night. It can't be ignored. Jump on or jump out of the way. Books — and their authors — make a statement.

For niche marketing that presumes you have followed the TCE process and have molded your book to meet a critical need of a targeted market, have customized it to their leaning and expectations, and have tested that market to see if the price and contents fit its buying taste. If not, you needn't do that unaided. I've published a book that hand-walks newcomers through the process in a detailed, step-by-step way: *Self-Publishing to Tightly-Targeted Markets.* (It's nearly as applicable for those having their book published by another house.)

How profitable are books?

In niche marketing, books can and should be extremely profitable if in fact you have properly identified a key need of your niche market, met it in the book, and have let that market's buyers know that your book exists, it meets a necessity, and how they can buy it.

In the first chapter we explained how you could write a book that showed dentists how to lower their malpractice insurance premiums 50%. In that example you saw about $180,000 in profit earned from the sale of 12,500 copies at $19.95 each, half of it in four weeks from the time the dentists were told, by flyer, that the book existed!

Later in the same example you saw that by applying that same basic format to six other professions similarly afflicted by malpractice insurance worries, then publishing books about that topic for each profession, another $400,000 profit could be earned.

Are niche marketed books profitable? You bet. The examples weren't woven of gossamer. They are replicable by you time and again.

The profit from books is sweeter because it is virtually without risk if the market is tested at least once — if in doubt, several times — to see that such a profit ratio exists before the book is written and printed.

We will discuss costs in the next segment but you could and should expect your profit to be at least half of the price you charge your buyer. That is, if the book costs $19.95 you should expect at least $10 of that to be profit.

Sweeter yet because almost all of that income is yours the moment the books are sold. Rarely would those in your niche market go to a bookstore or other selling outlet to buy your book. You will probably sell 75-90% of your books by direct mail, where orders, blessedly, are accompanied by cash, a check, or directly convertible credit card information — plus an additional amount for shipping, handling, and tax. If not, the book stays in your stock — or you voluntarily incur a risk by offering credit or absorbing shipping and other charges yourself.

Even if there is a bookstore or outlet where your book could be sold, with proper credit verification your payment is at very low risk, just delayed until the intermediate buyers pay the invoice, usually 30 days, though in the book world not uncommonly 60.

So the issue isn't profit per se. That is factored in the selling price. It's getting the buyer to make the purchase, which is a function of selling.

Which takes us back to the topic of the book — how crucial the need is and how well it is met — plus how effectively the curative power of your book is presented to those suffering the ailment: how well they are told that the book exists, how they can get it, and why they need it.

How much does it cost to use books as a niche selling means?

While the profit potential is high, the cost of producing books and maintaining a sensible inventory is also high, as is the usual method of marketing by direct mail. Worse, the costs are almost always due before the books can be sold: up-front.

So if it will cost you $50,000 to earn $100,000 gross (or $90,000 to earn $180,000 gross in the case of our book for dentists), your book only becomes possible to self-publish if you have that 50% starter money. Or you can devise a system to postpone some of the initial expenses. Or can get your market to buy your book in advance!

Let's look, then, at some of the specifics of our earlier example book, *Dentists: How to Lower Your Malpractice Insurance Premiums 50%*, to see what costs you might be able to reduce, which you might delay, or that you might even get paid by the book buyers before the text actually exists!

The book costs the buyer $19.95, who also pays shipping and tax. What kind of expenses might you incur in the preparation of this book, assuming you have a word processor but want the final text converted into a sharper camera-ready print image, and page-made, from your disk on a more advanced computer, and that your book is about 200 pages long, clothbound, and includes some line drawings and photos?

Your expenses might look like this:

Research, $1,500
Overhead, $500
Typesetting/board prep, $1,000
Cover preparation, $1,250
Proofing/editing, $1,000
Illustrations, $850
Printing ($3/book), $37,500
Delivery, $1,200
Other expenses, $1,000
Flyer prep, $1,800

TOTAL, $47,600

In addition, if this book is to be sold by mail you must print the flyer you have had artistically prepared, rent a mailing list, and have the flyers labeled and mailed. Let's say that costs 40 cents a flyer. If you sell this book to 10% of your market, you must add 10 x 40 cents, or $4 to each book for marketing costs.

Dividing the $47,600 above by the 12,500 books to be printed comes to $3.808 per book, plus $4 to get each book sold, and your cost is $7.808 per book. Half of $19.95 is $9.975, so you still have $2.167 per book more to spend if you are going to limit yourself to a 50% profit! (Or you could sell the book cheaper. But if the market wants it at $19.95, according to your testing, why not keep the higher profit and use it to finance the other means, like the newsletter or a tape series?)

Before moving on, you should know that the costs above are estimates and are probably high. See *Self-Publishing to Tightly-Targeted Markets* for a closer look at this process, plus a more detailed explanation of each step.

What of that $47,600 in preparation and production costs, plus the $4/book for mailing, then, might you be able to reduce? Or delay? Or get paid in advance?

Almost all of them could be lowered. You could typeset the book on your own laser printer, page-making it — preparing camera-ready boards — yourself, eliminating that $1,000 item. You could work with local editors and proofreaders, cutting that cost. Fewer illustrations. Bid the book out widely: $3 for a clothbound 200-page book in that quantity is very high. Sell by other means than direct mail. You must simply be careful not to trim so closely that the final book is unsalable to your niche buyers, not effectively marketed, or a book that so hurts your image people will not buy other items linked to your name.

Delaying some costs is also possible, but don't bet a pencil on it. You might get other professionals involved in the book's preparation or promotion — teletypsetters, cover artists, those involved in graphics or artwork, your proofreader, even the re-writer — to accept a later payment, once the book generates income. Or to be paid a percentage of the profits. Good luck.

One area has greater promise: get a printing contract that is payable 30 days after the book sees light. You will need excellent credit and usually a printing track record to get this, but it's worth pursuing. If your flyers are ready to send, or are sent, the day your book leaves the press, with 50% of the buyers responding within 30 days of receiving your selling material you should be able to pay at least that bill on time.

As for getting your niche market buyers to pay some of your expenses before the presses roll, or quickly thereafter, why not?

One way is to offer them a pre-pub special in your flyer. They will need a reason to take a risk, to pay in advance for a book yet to come. Part of the reason will be the critical worth of the book itself: their desire to have their need met as quickly as the information can reach their hands. Another will be the discount — or add-on — you will give them for paying before a certain date. It's said that 10% is the minimum discount you can offer to get purses and pockets opened; 20-25% will work better. Or 10% off and you will pay all tax and shipping. Or an additional report that expands upon some specific, gnarly side issue. Something. Buyers don't care that you're stretching to make them better or hardier or richer through your book. They need a reward to put their money in your pocket.

There's a potential trap here that must be avoided. Once you solicit an order and accept payment the postal authorities insist that the product be in the buyer's hands within 30 days. If not, you must inform them of the delay and offer their money back, which is burdensome and costly. On the other hand, if you state a date on which the book will be released, you can collect earlier, as long as it is in their possession within 30 days from the stated date. The point is obvious: be certain to hit your deadline — the announced release date — and get the books in the mail the moment they arrive!

You might generate some advance money through your flyer by offering to send other, purchased products or services immediately while they await the release of your book.

Another way is to announce the publication of a series of books which can be bought individually or, at a sizable discount, all at once. Use the payments for the series to finance the first edition, then the profits from it to underwrite subsequent editions. This carries greater risk, of course; and you must be sure to get the promised books out on time!

A fourth way to get some of the expenses paid close to the printing date is to have your book accepted by a book club. While it is fairly unlikely that there are many such clubs in niche subject areas, check the *Literary Market Place* in the library to see. If you find a firm that you think might be interested, follow the process explained in Poynter and Kremer's texts for selling to book clubs. For a book club to participate in your first printing, request that their portion of the printing be paid directly to the printer and the royalty be paid to you, both in 30 days. Then let the printer know what's up. That will lower the per-book printing and production costs and will get some fees-paying money in your hands.

Incidentally, while there are deviations, most book clubs pay you a set fee per book for production and printing plus 10% of the income from their buyers' purchases, which is often at a premium or sale price. For example, they might pay you $1.15 per $9.95 book plus $ .795 royalty on books they sell to their club members at $7.95. They also pay shipping from the printer to their warehouse.

A last, obvious way is to get somebody else to pay some or all of your expenses, in advance or quickly, for the privilege of distributing your book. While, again, this is unlikely for niched items, it is possible that a firm or an agency may wish to offer your book as a premium or promotional bait. You should be so lucky — or shrewd!

Are books a good "lead" means for niche marketing?

Books are probably the very best "lead" means in terms of making a statement and establishing you as "the" person to read, consult, or hire for further information about your niche topic. As I said earlier, your words in book form are permanent, reusable, verifiable — you cannot be taken lightly, unless the book proves you should be.

And books can be extraordinarily profitable.

Further, if you have developed other means that the book's readers would benefit from, such as tapes or reports, they can either be listed in the back of the book or on information sheets sent to those inquiring about or buying your book.

Books are a nearly endless pool or repository for articles. Parts of the book can be run in article form before its release, to stimulate interest. Other segments can then be used after publication, as they are, modified, expanded, or linked with some new fact or change.

Books serve as a core for subsequent books: the occasional update or revision, broken into follow-up segments by topic subdivisions, branched into spinoff topics, as a magnet for related articles for an anthology, a base for case studies, and more.

And if people in the niche market will pay to buy the book, why wouldn't they pay to receive current, related information from you in newsletter format? You have the names of all who bought the book and thus a valuable mailing list for newsletter promotion and subscription, as well as for other products.

But books are expensive to produce, must be printed in large quantities to offset the significant production and printing charges with resalable unit costs, and while niche books properly tested are low risk, there is still a fat parcel of money at stake.

So the answer to whether books are a good "lead" means for niche marketing is a huge "yes," but....

How are books best integrated with other means?

This question has largely been answered in the other segments, but let me once more attempt to mentally position books as a critical means of sharing niche information.

Because of the research required, the depth of content, and the care with which books are crafted they tend to be the pool where one fishes for information for the lesser, or less muscular, means, at least in terms of bulk. They bring the topic together into a sensible, orderly whole. Parts of that whole can then be caught, sometimes reconfigured, repackaged, and sold to those who abhor or haven't the time to pursue in-depth reading but will buy to see, listen, or glance at compacted fragments or smaller, new segments.

But sometimes it works the other way around. The fish are caught independently, drawn together, given order and words, and a book emerges!

That's a scaly analogy but you get the idea. Books are seldom more than a baby step from any of the other means, and are nearly always the mama of the baby.

Any final thoughts about books as niche marketing tools?

Resign yourself to it: if you're going to be the bearer of some particular core of knowledge, its creator or at least its contemporary guardian — if you are *the person* that any sensible person would seek to learn about it — you will almost certainly have to write a book. Don't despair. In Chapter 15 we will tell you how that can be done even if you can barely read and detest print.

Chapter 13C

Reports

I'd better define my use of the term "reports" first. They can run a wide gamut, from case studies to thick summary tables, from the most minute element studied in depth to the broadest overview. But I think of them as more than a flyer and less than a book that focuses on one very specific piece of information of critical interest to your niche market.

An example would be our report "100 Best Travel Newspaper Markets." It, typically, consists of a cover (with a heading, report title, byline, "Copyright 1992 by Gordon Burgett" line, and our company name, address, and phone/FAX); the cover backing (with a bibliography of travel-related books [ours and others'], our tapes, and our reports; ordering information, and a short biography of the report writer — in this case, me); seven pages total, two-sided, of instructions about how to sell travel articles (usually simultaneously) to newspapers in the United States; a blank page, and three final one-sided pages with 32 listings (travel editor by name, title and publication, address, and city, state, and ZIP) on each, in three columns, in Avery label format so the buyer can detach the sheets, take them to a fast-copy shop, and reproduce the information on pressure-sensitive labels.

This is a fictitious example of how one of those listings might appear:

Hector B. Smith
Travel Editor, Salem Spook
1357 Gossamer Street
Salem, MA 01234

Also, on the bottom of every text page — except the address sheets — I include a copyright reminder. In our case it reads this way: **All rights reserved by Communication Unlimited**.

No part of this report or study can be reproduced in any form or by any electronic or mechanical means including information storage and retrieval systems without written permission from the publisher. For reprint information, please contact Communication Unlimited, P.O. Box 6405, Santa Maria, CA 93456. (This is a standard warning that I plucked from elsewhere. Use it if you wish — just put your name in place of ours!)

One of my primary niche markets is writers: I tell them how they can sell their articles, books, and sundry spinoffs. Since more than half my writing has been travel-related, those are the examples I have used in my seminars and books. I also recently wrote a book specially for travel writers called *The Travel Writer's Guide*.

So, after explaining at least 100 times to others how difficult it was to know which newspaper travel editors are buying freelance, how to find their names and addresses, and how to use that information, it struck me that I could provide that material in a specific report and add a list of the 100 top buying travel editors, updated on Sept. 1 every year. The Avery label concept was easy: that's what we did, compiling our own list and copying it for our use.

In other words, we were doing the tedious compilation anyway. Why not add some explanation to our data and make it available annually? (Why did it take me a couple of years to identify this obvious aid and profit center? Realization that we had missed a good opportunity for far too long was one of the things, in truth, that prompted me to write this book, so your coffers — and those in need in your niche area — don't lose those years, or even months.)

How do we sell that report? Mainly at the back-of-the-room product sale after seminars. About 80% of those B.O.R. sales come after the "Writing Travel Articles That Sell!" program; almost all of the rest, at other writing seminars.

That number is matched by mail order purchases: from our catalog, passalong sales from our seminar order forms, word-of-mouth buyers (usually friends of earlier buyers), responses to direct mail flyers featuring *The Travel Writer's Guide*, an order form in the back of that book, and other, mysteriously lucrative means (that is, I have no idea whatsoever).

What is the best way to use reports for niche marketing?

One very good — maybe the best — way to use reports is to supplement other, established means to sell more of your expertise. Like selling a working list of U.S. travel editors to travel writing seminar participants who just learned why they need precisely that information!

Another example puts a spin on this. For about a decade I've been offering a seminar (now tape) program called "How to Set Up and Market Your Own Seminar." For a while I also gave a four-part follow-up seminar that addressed, for an hour each, the four items that seminar-givers most wanted to know more about: how to create and sell workbooks or booklets (like those they had to prepare as seminar handouts), how to develop and sell their own mailing lists (starting with attendees at their seminars), how to sell products back of the room at their presentations, and how to produce and sell their own audiocassettes (including tapes of their seminars).

That seminar didn't draw well because the focus was too scattered: some wanted this, others that, but not enough were eager to sit through it all. And it was hard to title, which is very important when the programs are primarily sold through fat but finely-honed catalogs from universities.

So I broke it into other means better suited to limited information than seminars or books. Our best-selling single audiocassette is one result: appropriately, "Producing and Selling Your Own Audio Cassette." For six years the mailing list information was also sold by tape. And the workbook production was merged into a larger seminar, now a two-part program, about self-publishing. It also is again seeing light in the words you are now reading since an excellent use for workbooks is as reports.

But one fourth of that ill-fated seminar still survives, very profitably, in actual report form: "Generating Back-of-the-Room Sales." It began as a single audiocassette, and still partly exists in a specialty tape by that name directed to consultants.

Again, a report is an ideal way to take a limited but important piece of information, isolate it, focus fully on it, and sell it as a separate, valuable product.

How profitable are reports?

They can be extremely profitable, marginally so, or a great way to generate customers while more than paying for themselves and their promotion. Which of those three depends upon two things: (1) how much you charge and (2) why you are offering them, or how they fit into your larger mix.

Reports aren't expensive to produce. If you use a fancy cover, meaning thicker and classier paper and perhaps some visionary logo or design, that may cost 10-15 cents apiece. If the contents are two-sided, figure about a dime a page. (If you want to travel on the high road, single-sided reports are it: more pages, 5-7 cents each. Also more bulk to ship.) The report must be collated and stapled: a penny or two more. Or punched and bound with brads or holders, at perhaps 4-10 cents each. Or fancier binding yet.

A 20-pager like ours (two-sided, simple cover, stapled) costs $1.20 tops. That presumes that you produce them as needed, 10-20 at a time, at a good copy shop. If you need hundreds or thousands, you can up the quality of the cover and binding and still pay well below that.

A second blessing emerges: you need maintain a very small inventory. In fact, you could have your reports on disk and produce them singly, as requested, keeping only a supply of stock printed covers which are filled in, by the computer, with that report's name and copyright date.

A significant part of the initial expense hasn't been mentioned, though. That is, the words that contain your idea and information. Framing the concept; reading the related sources; gathering the facts, quotes, and anecdotes; massaging those into clear, intelligent prose; getting that proofed, and putting the final report into camera-ready (or computer-ready) form simply takes time, energy, and footwork (which is mostly rumpwork).

Which costs. Yet that is what our kind of niche marketing sells, so without the information and the travail of organizing and presenting it you have no product at all. The nice thing is that one morsel of information, well structured and packaged, can sell in that form — as a report, book, tape, whatever — for a long, long time.

But not always, which suggests more costs. Not all information stays fresh and fully applicable forever as it is initially sold.

So sometimes you must update reports: once, occasionally, or regularly.

The concept and techniques of "Generating Back-of-the-Room Sales" has changed so little in the six years it has existed as a report that I have only redone it once, mainly to tighten up the writing.

On the other hand, the "100 Best Travel Newspaper Markets" change weekly — travel editors die (only those who buy often and pay wildly) or are fired (the nonbuyers too rarely), newspapers get glutted or go broke and temporarily pull out of the freelance market, sometimes publications even change addresses — so here an annual update is mandatory.

Alas, more costs in creating updated reports can mean more income too: last year's list isn't nearly as usable this year and is a liability next year. Niche customers in need will want to buy the newest version.

Profits? It depends upon how much you can charge — and why you are offering the reports in the first place.

If you are working the business route, what you have to say in one report will earn the buyer many thousands of dollars, it is unique material in this format, and they already know you as a solid, reliable source, you might charge $200.

But if you're working the writers' route, who, however lovely and creative they are as people, cherish every dime as if it were minted in their name, you are lucky to get an extra $5 for true report magic. (Their logic: hell, they can get a full paperback, hundreds of pages and weeks of before-bed reading pleasure, for that same $5!) That is why all of my reports cost $6 each and are detailed, current applications of information initially presented in one of my books or at a seminar. They know the contact source is solid (they just read the book or heard the seminar), they know that the additional information is valuable, it will save them far more time or earn them greater profit than the report costs, and it's readily available: buy it after the presentation or call/FAX/write at the number/address indicated.

So profits are relative. If I produced a $200 report that cost me $2.50 to prepare (with the buyer paying the postage and tax) and I sold 100 copies, that would bring in a sweet $19,750. At $6 and a prep cost of $1.20, selling 100, a modest profit of $480. Often, it's about as easy to sell one as the other.

If you too work a price-sensitive market you might be inclined, now, to skip to another section after seeing only $480 as the reward per report. Stay here a bit longer. In 1992 we earned just a pinch under $5,000 from eight different reports, up 27% in a recessionary year from 1991. But reports are just one of our 14 income categories — and they are flat-out tag-on money. Rarely do we sell just one report. At least 95% of our orders include one or several key items, from $9.95-$44.95, to which a report is added on. Which says to me that without the reports our profit margin would be at least $4,000 lower — plus the potential lost sale of many of the larger items where the report first lured them our way. Our niche market buyers would also have been far less informed and aided.

What that might say is that reports, while usually not good leader items nor high profit boomers, can sensibly be produced to fatten up your overall profit margin while expanding your spread in the buyers' niche field. With reports, there is more of you filling more needs — some more profitable, others less — but in total you pose a more significant presence and earn a grander return.

Another important point regarding reports and profits. There is no discount paid to an intermediate seller. With books, if sold through distributors, you lose up to 55% of the list price. Almost anything you sell through a store costs you 40%. But reports are so intimately tied to the sale of your other niche items, which in turn are seldom sold through stores or intermediaries, that you earn 100% of the selling price. In other words, that $19,750 (or $480) is yours, period. And well earned.

There's the reverse side to profits: losses. They should be minimal in the case of reports. Even if you fail to sell one copy of your first 100, you have lost only a few hundred dollars at most, since initially they will be advertised or promoted only as an adjunct to, or with, larger ticket items. You'd be smarter to produce even fewer than 100 at the inception, to further reduce that long-shot loss possibility. Even the text preparation isn't lost. Either sell it as is, or subdivided, as an article or articles or, if appropriate, modify it into a cassette script. Or both!

Are reports a good "lead" means for niche marketing?

Seen from the profit angle, probably not, since the profit, in most cases, from each report will be modest. Certainly not where the cost of the report must be low.

Another thing mitigates against reports as lead items, particularly those sold at low prices: the promotional costs to put a lead item in front of your niche market. A rough rule of thumb is a return of 3:1 from advertising, so you want to earn at least $15 for every $5 you spend to make that sale.

If the report sells for $6, $4.80 of which is profit, and it costs $3 to sell, how will you ever earn enough to keep bread on the table? You'd have to sell hundreds of thousands! But if the report sells for $49, costs $2.50 to produce, and it costs $10 to sell, gold dust — if you sell in quantity.

Yet a case can be made for leading with a report, if it is quickly followed by more substantial means to take advantage of the initial impact and buying draw your report creates.

If a sudden, critical need were to arise in your niche field that could be handled directly, clearly, and fully by a report, one could justify putting a hefty price tag on it, broadcasting its availability to the market, and getting it into the buyers' hands by overnight express, modem, or FAX.

An example with appeal. A blight hits the banana crop, you know a quick and certain remedy, and it can be explained in report length. Go to it. All the better if you sell plant nostrums that can be used now or after the cure. Then provide more and stouter materials needed by that banana clientele, branching out into the other information dissemination means, selling first to those wise enough to buy your quick cure (and thus are on your mailing list). Write the banana growers' manual, slip in a newsletter, speak to their gatherings, create other reports....

The key point here: its cost is high enough to profitably promote, it is desperately needed, and you can follow up with other, related niche items that solidify your presence.

How are reports best integrated with other means?

They are perfect spinoffs from other means. To return to our example, I explain how to sell articles simultaneously to newspaper travel editors in a book or a seminar, which are designed to explain broader procedural concepts over several years, then I provide, in a report, a current list, in reproducible fashion, of 100 of the best buyers of those same newspaper travel editors every year.

You can even create spinoffs of spinoffs. As this book is being written my company is first offering a report in identical fashion called "100 Best Canadian Magazine/Newspaper Travel Markets," by A. Carroll Burgess! Note that we have commissioned somebody else to draw from her expertise to serve our niche field, and we will pay her a royalty on all of her reports that we sell. While we were at it, she will be selling our report in Canada and paying us the same royalty!

And if the Canadian list sells well enough, we are considering something similar for English-written freelance markets outside the U.S. and Canada. All updated annually. Plus we are exploring hot-ticket, shorter updates. And converting some or all of these to computer.

You can highlight segments from a book and provide current information via reports. A book about OSHA regulations might describe the philosophy, with examples. But updates as they relate to your niche market might require an annual, or even monthly, report(s) of all changes that are pertinent, plus specific case studies as needed.

The same might apply to seminars, where you provide in the base time allocated all of the procedures or information possible, but relegate specific details to reports.

Or that function might better be shared by the other formats we discuss in this book: a newsletter might be more effective, less costly, and more profitable. So might single audiocassettes, for those preferring to hear the information or who have a better opportunity to hear the tape while commuting or traveling. Or an article in a widely read publication if you also wish to draw quick attention to yourself as an expert in the field.

You see how quickly and easily information and ideas move from one format to another, finding their optimum and final resting spot in the means best suited to the market's needs and habits? Since my niche markets consist of written-word folk (writers mostly) and oral-based learners (usually speakers), we often produce our products in two forms at the outset — reports or books and tapes or seminars — until either one format prevails or both do. Then we spin off further into related tapes and reports.

Again, the report of 100 best newspaper travel markets is an excellent example. It began as a seminar for travel writers, which came from my original seminar (now a book), *How to Sell 75% of Your Freelance Writing*. From the travel writing seminar came the book, *The Travel Writer's Guide*. From that came the "100 Best..." report, and from that are now coming the other spinoffs just mentioned.

But it can work in reverse too. Before I wrote *The Travel Writer's Guide*, it became obvious to me, when offering the travel writing seminar, that while I could show the participants how to sell their manuscripts about traveling topics, many of them didn't know what to look for or write about once they arrived at a new site. So I wrote a report called "300 Ideas for Travel Articles," giving them a wide choice of rather generic but suitable topics they might find in Addis Ababa, Albuquerque, or Aden.

Then, when I wrote the book, I included the report in the appendix, since it was germane to the theme. (We still offer it as a report for those who, for some peculiar reason, don't want to buy the book.) Then we took the orders of all those who had bought the report before the book was published, sent each buyer a flyer telling how the book would show them how to sell copy about the ideas in the report, and sold at least 100 more books! (At $14.95 each that's almost $1500 income for less than $100 expenditure just by tracing backwards.)

The concept carries through to this very book. For about a year, in preparation for putting these ideas together and as a spinoff from my book *Self-Publishing to Tightly-Targeted Markets,* I offered a report called "100 Topic Ideas for Niche Marketed Books." Modified, that is Chapter Six in this text, since it too is central to this topic. And yes, I will contact those who bought that report and tell them that this book will help them put those ideas in motion in an even larger context!

The purpose here is not to show you how clever I am. I could better show you a hundred dumb things I did that I don't want you to do. Nor has it been, in this segment, to unduly display my products, except to use them as examples of how reports might work best for you.

Rather, I want to show you that all of the information dissemination formats, niche-driven, are closely related, and that reports are one of the less risky, potentially more profitable means by which ideas and information can be defined, explained, and sold, alone or in conjunction with the other, usually more complex means.

Any final thoughts about reports as niche marketing tools?

Unless the situation is just right and the price you can get is high enough, don't dwell long on reports at the outset. Get established, let others in your niche market see you through books, seminars, or the splashier and more profound means, then spin off key, timely elements by report — if your market will buy reports and that makes economic sense given the time and energy report offering requires.

Chapter 13D

Newsletters

Why would I even dare suggest that those four-page, typed, mimeographed throwaways ground out by groups like the Bug Institute or Master Muldoon's School for Malcontents might play a key part in your march toward indispensability, immortality, and monetary munificence? Because, according to F.D. Goss, the Executive Director of The Newsletter Association, "(they are) the most pervasive type of printed publication in the world."

Moreover, like bacteria in petri dishes, newsletters thrive in obscure, niched areas but lose their power the wider they are broadcast. Hundreds of thousands of them earn anywhere from hundreds of millions to $3 billion annually.

The 1991 *Oxbridge Directory of Newsletters* adds: "This is the age of the newsletter. And it's easy to see why. Today technology is moving at the speed of light.... Magazines aren't timely enough to keep up. But newsletters can. Simply produced, quickly distributed, they bring their readers new ideas fast, (w)hile they're still fresh enough to be useful and profitable. Magazines are general; newsletters can be highly specialized and specific." So I'd be remiss, if not foolish, not to give them their due on these pages, particularly since they can be an excellent means of solidifying your expertise, making yourself damn near essential in your field, and much richer while you're at it.

But they can also be a colossal waste of time and money, a labyrinthine diversion from more appropriate and profitable forms of niche marketing, a trap easily entered but tarnishingly escaped.

In other words, at some point you will probably have to seriously consider offering your own newsletter. But you also should do it with your mind and eyes very wide open, your purpose writ-

ten out, your selling universe fully researched and accessible —
all with extra time and money set aside, at hand and ready to be
applied with conviction.

Howard Penn Hudson is the guru of newsletters, the niche
king, and his book *Publishing Newsletters: A Complete Guide to
Markets, Editorial Content, Design, Subscriptions, Management,
and Desktop Publishing*, in the revised 1988 edition, is still the
book to read before you invest a dime.

Let me draw primarily from it and paint an overview of
what newsletters are (and aren't) before we consider this means
in the more specific, niche marketing context of this book.

In the grandest sense newsletters are subscription publications without ads that can't be found for sale on newsstands. Nor
are they accessible in many libraries.

Except that many of them aren't exactly, or directly, sold by
subscription. Many are paid for by dues. And lots of them are
absolutely free, and some do include ads.

I particularly like Hudson's criterion of differentiation.
"Whatever their physical appearance, there is one unifying char-
acteristic of newsletters: *they provide specialized information*
(italics are his). They are informal publications, created to serve
designated audiences or universes rather than a mass audience.
Many times the audience served is a narrow segment of a universe that wants information in depth."

What do they look like? Usually 8 1/2 x 11" in size and 4-8
pages long, probably monthly or bimonthly, coverless and pho-
toless, written the full width of the page (or occasionally two or
three columns wide), typed or set in Courier font, underlining
permitted, mimeographed or photo offset, sometimes three-hole
punched for binders, probably on 60-pound paper. With lots of
deviations, most stylistically caused by the use of desktop publishing.

What do they cost, if there's a charge at all? Hudson cites
the median subscription price in a 1987 survey of the publications listed in *Hudson's Newsletter Directory* as $95.50. At that
time 26 of those newsletters were priced at $1,000 or more, with
the *Video Marketing Surveys and Forecasts* tops at $4,500. (It
still charged $4,500 in 1991.)

And to whom are newsletters sold? In the subscription division, Hudson lists five principal categories: investment letters, business letters, consumer newsletters, affinity newsletters, and instructional newsletters. In the nonsubscription category, five more kinds of newsletters: association, organizational, corporate, franchise, and public relations.

Even more important to us, he offers an excellent insight into the price/value component of subscription newsletter marketing through the use of "Hudson's Pyramid." A triangular pyramid is divided into four sections, each separated from the section below it by a horizontal line. At the peak is the business segment. Next down is the affinity segment, followed, in descending order, by organizations and consumers. These represent the adult population in America.

Even though the business group at top is by far the smallest numerically it is also, again by far, the most eager to buy solid, condensed, usable information without undue concern for its cost, since its purchase is a business expense. Businesses seek and readily pay for information they need.

The affinity segment shares a common interest in something like a sport, hobby, or avocation. They need specific information about their shared interest that they can't get from the mass media or elsewhere. They will buy newsletters to get it but will pay less because the expense is from their own pocket.

Organizations of all kinds ply their members with magazines, reports, and nonsubscription newsletters so those members are a poor source for subscriptions to additional newsletters. But the leaders of the organizations have their own peculiar needs, not unlike other businessfolk — about trends, government actions, goods and services for the members — and they will dip into the limited budget and pay for newsletters. But not much.

And consumers, meaning everybody (including those in segments just mentioned but here "out of uniform"), will pay the least, if anything at all. Most don't value information enough to want to pay for it, they are already deluged by free newsletters (or handouts that look like newsletters), any cost seems outlandish for a piece of paper only a few pages long — and it costs you a ton just to find the few who might subscribe.

There is one more thing that must be asked here: what do newsletters contain that will coax $95.50 (or even $4,500) a year from enough subscribers to see what is on those few pages? Goss says newsletters "convey ... some combination of insider news, detailed analysis, industry gossip, pricing information, how-to suggestions, esoteric knowledge, opinionated editorial, or straight hard-news reporting." To which Hudson adds, they are often subscribing to buy your mind about what is new, important, worth additional time reading or discussing. Plus what you think of it. Here you can editorialize in the text; they are buying you, your thoughts, and the information all in the same package.

What is the best way to use newsletters for niche marketing?

As a logical follow-up to one or several expertise-establishing penetrations into your niche field.

Define what core of knowledge or information you want to be the expert on, for which niche group (at least initially), and then put yourself and your expertise most forcefully before them.

Said another way, define your objective, line up your forces, strike the camp, and attack.

A book or a seminar is often the most effective first thrust: it (and the promotion announcing it) puts you before your niche field with a needed product that can be directly evaluated. Those who count in your field will quickly know whether you are or aren't a worthy expert. If you are, you move out, you spread and expand your expertise by other means.

Newsletters are a logical consideration. They are also expensive in terms of outlay and time, which can mean that they overwhelm the other means and become the primary and sometimes only way you maintain your expertise.

There are two very persuasive reasons for letting other means precede newsletters. The first is that by leading with a book or seminar you will be able to test the strength of interest in your expertise by your niche field: do they care enough to pay to read or hear what you have to say? If they don't care enough to buy a book or attend a seminar, chances are formidable that they won't want to pay for a newsletter subscription, particularly a hefty one!

The second reason relates to identifying the central buying core of your niche market. By selling a product to your larger buying universe and putting the purchasers on your own mailing list, if they benefited from the initial product, it is likely they will consider buying more information about that same product, from you, in newsletter form. That starting nucleus of dedicated, buying followers is invaluable.

So you use newsletters to bring those who already accept your expertise, or at least want to know more about your subject, into your orb on a continuous basis, and you meet their need through a newsletter format: providing specialized information, analysis, opinion, news, updates on research, "inside" scuttlebutt — whatever it is that your newsletter does.

Are newsletters a good "lead" means for niche marketing?

No, for the reasons just stated.

Could you make your splash — your debut adorned in singular expertise — through a newsletter? You could, but it seems to me that it would be extremely risky: expensive and a huge commitment devoid of the requisite and prudent fundament.

You would launch a subscription drive offering to sell special knowledge in a field where the experts and leaders are probably known. You aren't, but nonetheless you want the niche buyers' money — a fair chunk of it — to buy some sheets of paper every month or so that will in some way improve their lives, increase their profit, or whatever.

Your appeal will be as vague as that last statement. Targets of your subscription flyer will surely ask themselves:

"Who is this person?"
"Why should I buy from him/her?"
"What do they know that I don't? And even if they
do know something, can they continue to provide
anything new and worthwhile for a full year?"
"What else could I do with that much money?"

No doubt they will find something better to do with their funds than subscribe, and be reassured of their wisdom when your newsletter never sees the light of day for want of buyers.

Even if you are successful and do manage to lure in enough subscribers, about the only thing worse than having no newsletter is having a full year's commitment to provide a newsletter to a very small, tenuous readership, many of whom simply won't renew. Then you must bail out, unless another expensive subscription drive dredges up some replacements. Your best hope is that you prove yourself through another means — probably a book or seminar — while the newsletter continues, pulling in a sizable new hunk of subscribers from that display of expertise. So why not do that first and start the newsletter from a much stronger base?

What you want to avoid is starting a newsletter that folds. Better not to start at all. Best to wait until you have a following eager to hear or read your next word, then provide it by that means.

How profitable are newsletters? And how much does it cost to use newsletters as a niche selling means?

Newsletters can be very profitable indeed. But the money doesn't just waft in, to be blown on frills. You earn every nickel — and very often spendable profits don't really occur until you've survived the first year, renewals are assured, the second subscription campaign worked, and you are well above a 5% sales rate to your targeted niche field.

Let's set up two examples (on the next page) to show how newsletter funds must be spent, what leads to financial success, and where profit might occur. I'm borrowing the format (from James J. Marshall) and a percentage from Howard Penn Hudson, again from *Publishing Newsletters.*

Let's say there are two niche marketers interested in offering newsletters to their universes. One, to match our earlier example, serves dentists of which there are some 125,000 reachable by list. The other serves a market of 20,000. Both monthlies, the dental newsletter will cost $65 a year; the other, $120.

Hudson suggests that an arbitrary response rate to a subscription mailing might be 1.5%, but that you should reach 5% in two to three years. So let's use 1.5% for one comparison. Yet I think niche marketers as we have described them in this book, already established as experts in their field through other means, should quickly be at 10%. Thus let me use my own arbitrary number of 7% in response to a mixed subscription mailing to both a general list of nichefolk plus your own list of buyers of your other products, like a book or a registration for a seminar. I have indicated how I arrived at the other tallies in the table on the next page by each classification; they should be adjusted as needed for your calculations.

NEWSLETTER				
Universe	125,000	125,000	20,000	20,000
Subscription price	$65	$65	$120	$120
Frequency	Monthly	Monthly	Monthly	Monthly
Response rate	1.5%	1.5%	7%	7%
# Subscribers	1,875	8,750	300	1,400
INCOME/YEAR	$121,875	$568,750	$36,000	$168,000
PROMOTIONAL COSTS	(1 mailing)			
Printing (20 cents @)	$25,000	$25,000	$4,000	$4,000
Postage (bulk, 16.7 cents @)	$20,875	$20,875	$3,340	$3,340
Mailing charges ($37/1000)	$4,625	$4,625	$740	$740
List rental ($50/1000)	$6,250	$6,250	$1,000	$1,000
TOTAL PROMOTION	$56,750	$56,750	$9,080	$9,080
EXPENSES				
Printing	$5,625 (.25@)	$17,850 (.17@)	$1,980 (.55@)	$5,040 (.30 @)
Postage (12.4 cents @)	$2,790	$13,020	$446	$2,083
Billings ($3/year)	$5,625	$26,250	$900	$4,200
Overhead (editorial)	$10,000	$10,000	$10,000	$10,000
TOTAL EXPENSES	$24,040	$67,120	$13,326	$21,323
INCOME	$121,875	$568,750	$36,000	$168,000
PROMOTION + EXPENSES	$80,790	$123,870	$22,406	$30,403
PROFIT/LOSS	$41,085	$444,880	$13,594	$137,597

107

The most important elements in newsletters are the printed words. Without them, what have you to sell? Behind those words comes your special expertise, otherwise the words are no different from those written by any other literate person. Then to make it a worthwhile venture in terms of energy, time, and profit, you need readers eager enough to pay to see what you say — and satisfied enough to do that year after year.

Yet the income/expense analysis sheet puts a different spin on it. For conventional newsletters, where a 1.5% subscription response might be expected, your promotional costs far exceed your production costs, even factoring in $10,000 as editorial overhead.

Where you begin as a recognized expert, rewarded on this table with a 7% subscription response, the promotional costs are still sizable — but a far less significant part of the gross income.

Are newsletters expensive? In sheer dollars, even our most modest example, 300 copies sent monthly, the costs are $22,406. That soars to $123,870 for 8,750 copies.

Where the tougher costs occur is in the time spent not only designing the newsletter and arranging for its production — not to mention the creation of promotional material, its distribution, and handling the replies — but in gathering, verifying, writing, proofing, and graphically producing the crucial text.

Many of the mechanical elements of newsletter preparation and promotion can be farmed out, of course, wholly or piecemeal, but if you are using this vehicle to promote your expertise in the niche field, that takes your attention, flexibility finding new copy every issue, sometimes courage in saying what must be said, and a commitment for the long haul. Newsletters aren't flags to fly solely on sunny days. They are yearlong, decade-long pledges not undertaken lightly just to bolster the bottom line or see yourself in print when you get around to it. The point is that there are costs, in dollars, and costs in performance and commitment.

As to the specific steps one takes to create a profitable newsletter, I again direct you to Hudson's excellent text, *Publishing Newsletters: A Complete Guide to Markets, Editorial Content, Design, Subscriptions, Management, and Desktop Publishing,* the newest version.

To see what other newsletters exist in your niche area, consult the most recent issue of both the *Oxford Directory of Newsletters* and the *Standard Directory of Newsletters.* Herman Holtz wrote a hard-to-find book called *The Consultant's Guide to Newsletter Profits* in 1987, and I have found useful, in a general way, an earlier (1982) primer by Mark Beach called *Editing Your Newsletter.*

How are newsletters best integrated with other means?

You know by now that I encourage their creation, if at all, after you have made your presence and specialness known to your niche market.

When after is up to you. I should think that at the point where you have others clamoring to know more, you are unable to meet that demand in person, and there is simply much left to say that they want to get from you, it would be logical that you offer that unique information to all at the same time in as personal a way as possible, through a newsletter.

The newsletter can be promoted through your seminars or speeches, in a product sheet in the back of your book, referred to on your cassettes, highlighted in the sales material you send with each purchase or by direct mail. In short, use all of your contacts to make its existence and uniqueness known.

The newsletter itself can be a font of other income. You might include classified ads limited to your niche field, though the buyers must know of this in advance since they will presume the newsletter is ad-free.

You will naturally mention your own products in the text, and you can mail a product sale sheet with the newsletter to facilitate buying. You can also expand that product sheet to include others' books and items that you endorse as being useful to those in your niche field. In fact, that could expand to a catalog, which could be a different income source altogether, using the newsletter mailing list at the inception — and including, of course, your newsletter in the catalog!

Any thoughts about nonsubscription newsletters?

Yes. But first let me remind you that what I'm otherwise addressing in this section are paid subscription newsletters.

The free variety — newsletters, fact sheets, information fly-ers — that you send to your niche market can be very effective, can continue to position you as an expert, and can help promote you and your products.

I think the kind that work best are almost identical in struc-ture to subscription newsletters: factual, to the point, full of vital information, and devoid of any self-promotion altogether. They can be accompanied by catalogs or order forms but the fact sheet doesn't sell anything at all.

The next best kind blend the above with occasional inserts about new products you are launching, comments or updates on earlier products, whatever.

Their effectiveness in positioning you is directly related to how the recipient perceives this unexpected mail item. If they see it as junk mail thinly wrapped in a few facts, it — and a pinch of your good will — gets tossed. Better to send a flat-out advertisement done in ad form to achieve a selling purpose.

But if the recipient will read it, set it aside to finish later, and be grateful for its contents, it's probably worth the time spent putting it together and mailing it. Nothing wrong with your name and photo prominently displayed either. Or so it seems to me. I'm very impressed by people who have something valuable to say, share it openly, and don't expect to get anything back for doing so. Flyers of that nature have the same effect.

Any final thoughts about newsletters as niche marketing tools?

My ambivalence about newsletters is more than theoretical. I was on the verge of launching just such a vessel about seminar-ing in California some years back, even announced it and re-ceived a few subscriptions, when I took one final look at the time it would take in comparison to the other means I could use to achieve a similar impact. I bailed out as quick as I could!

For me the timing was wrong, the commitment was luke-warm, and my funds were stretched thin for a new venture that risky.

Yet as I review the potential profit and talk with others I see that newsletters can be an absolutely ideal, and very lucrative, way to nail down one's expertise, share it over the long haul, and make a steady, continual impact in any area that you love.

You simply must look at those numbers yourself, weigh the commitment, and make your own decision. Just don't lead with a newsletter. It's a super second or third punch, methodically prepared, then wholeheartedly thrown.

"On speech-making: If you don't strike oil in 20 minutes, stop boring."

Andrew Carnegie (1835-1919)

Chapter 14

Niche Marketing by Speaking

Talks and Speeches

Talks and speeches sound the same to the outsider but there's a huge difference if you're giving them for a living: talks are free, speeches are paid! Speakers may say the very same thing, but a talk — however inspiring, lifesaving, or truly world changing it is — is just so much hot air. A speech, in a manner of speaking, is edible.

Professional speakers, who make their living by orating, give speeches for which they are paid, and sometimes talks, when overcome by charity or trying to generate speeches.

There is a sense of progression in the trade: speakers usually master their skills by talking to groups that don't pay, can't, or wouldn't to hear their message: PTA's, service clubs, women's lunch gatherings, church organizations, and hundreds more. Those are tough listeners who demand to be both informed and entertained, the two things that successful speakers must do.

Once the talkers feel ready, have something to say that others (usually corporations, associations, or larger organizations) will pay to have their members hear, and have sufficient acumen to handle the business and logistical components, they offer their message for sale, and if bought the talkers become paid speakers.

What is the best way to use talks and speeches for niche marketing?

These are excellent lead items. If you have some core of information you feel that others want to or should hear about, just get in front of them and talk. The talking isn't hard. You can or you can't. If you can, it's the "getting in front of them" that takes almost all of your time — particularly if you want to be handsomely recompensed for declaiming.

Since we're specifically addressing niche topics in this book, you know the kinds of listeners who would benefit from hearing your words. Determine when they receive information in a speech format. Do they have local or regional meetings where speakers appear, or could? Conventions? Gatherings of any kind?

If so, find the person in charge of planning the meeting, tell them of your availability and how your information meets the attendees' needs (or why you think they would benefit from hearing you), and simply get booked. Then speak so well that the listeners froth with anticipation at receiving more good information from you. So that they can indeed act upon that bubbling enthusiasm, put something in their hands — a flyer reminding them of the five key points, a summary, a related (often humorous) sheet defining terms or concepts, even an order form for your products. If that's impossible, refer to a way that you can be reached so listeners can see or get your address and/or phone number; the more enthusiastic can reach you for more facts, inspiration, or guidance.

Sometimes your products might be available or on display where you are speaking. Invite your audience over to meet you personally at your booth or exhibition, where you can distribute promotional material and give out business cards.

But the speech itself is your best selling tool. Nothing works so well to galvanize or create a following than having vital information passionately presented. Well done, it proves that the topic is important, you are an expert, and you have the skills of a leader. Nor will anything more quickly bring a fervid pack to a thunderous peak, on their feet applauding and shouting their approval.

Even audiences that sit on their hands are reached at an emotional level, while intellectually processing the words. That is hard to attain by any other means. Writing brings the same words; audiocassettes, the same sound; videocassettes bring both but lack the involvement. Being there, hearing and seeing and directly participating, put speaking on a unique plateau in the niche marketing field.

Having said that, nothing will work as quickly in reverse either. Ramble about something ill-defined or unimportant, say nothing with great bravado, flail and emote about foolishness and why would anybody want to read, hear, or experience more of you and your nonsense?

If you talk to a small gathering, the damage is contained. They paid nothing and got their money's worth. But give a paid speech and you're in trouble. Meeting planners share horror stories. And spurned audiences never forget.

How profitable are talks and speeches?

On the surface, talks aren't profitable at all. You aren't paid, lest it be a half-warm meal or a pen set. As often, you pay to get there, park, and sometimes even to register. You suspect that the time alone could be better spent doing something else, like marketing.

But on the other hand, if you are properly positioning yourself as an expert, as the person to solve specific problems or overcome frustrations or just get answers, and the audience includes enough listeners so that the knowledge of your expertise will be spread and/or responses will be generated, the profits can be large. Profits cashed later.

That is particularly the case at conventions and professional gatherings where your perception as an expert to your niche field, or a related field, can be invaluable — well worth the out-of-pocket costs incurred to make that impression.

The second time talks can be justified is when you are using them to master your speaking skills. At that stage, if possible, it's better that your listeners be from fields afar. Akin to learning to play third base as a kid in Keokuk before you try out in Chicago. Better they see you polished and professional when you hit the big leagues, undistracted by memories of you trying to field your shoe in seventh grade!

An excellent training field is provided by Toastmasters, where you get to practice with peers, who will critique you on the spot. Check the phone book or the Chamber of Commerce to find the branch nearby. From them, move on to the local organizations. Let me offer a suggestion. When you are ready, contact a local charity that is doing yeoman work, volunteer to speak for it, then learn all you can about it. The United Fund, for example. See what they are doing, talk with the workers, sit in on sessions, get to know recipients of their aid. Gather relevant facts, quotes, and anecdotes and work them into a dandy, honest, moving, and entertaining short speech. Then ask local service and social groups if you can talk to their members for 10-15 minutes at their next meeting. The results are all positive. Everybody wins. And you're ready to convert your newfound skills to marketing to your own niche.

Professional speaking — talking for money — can be very profitable, particularly if it's about your niche topic and the income is augmented by product and service sales, directly after the speech or later.

Speakers often start charging in the low hundreds of dollars, rise fairly quickly into the low thousands (where speaking bureaus become interested in booking them), and often settle in the $2500-5000/speech range. Some double that, and a few — often celebrities — can command even considerably more. Speeches usually last from 30-60 minutes, with keynotes paying tops and lasting the longest. Additional payment is made for round-trip transportation, room, board, and incidentals, though some speakers include all costs other than lodging in their fee.

Some speakers offer a more comprehensive package: on-site preparation, a warmup talk at the opening of the session(s), sometimes the introduction of the CEO, occasionally a seminar or workshop, the keynote, and even the closing. They sometimes offer an article or some short pieces related to their presentation theme for use in the sponsor's newsletter in advance of the presentation.

Ralph Archbold, when hired to speak as Benjamin Franklin to gatherings, often includes visits to local schools in his fee. Others, speaking about overcoming physical obstacles, include hospital and recovery unit visits as part of their package.

Sometimes a sponsor will want to tape the presentation. If that is to be used in a money-earning capacity, the rights sale can increase the speaker's fee. So can back-of-the-room sales, though those are more often made at seminars (discussed in the next section of this chapter).

At times the sponsor will purchase a lump quantity of the speaker's book for distribution to the audience, which can also increase the speaker's income, sizably if the book is self-published. (It's always better to have these books distributed well before or after the speech lest the audience be noisily leafing through and reading while you are earnestly emoting!)

The best way to learn professional marketing techniques for speakers is to join the National Speakers Association. Contact them at 1500 S. Priest Drive, Tempe, AZ 85281/(602) 968-2552. Since it's expensive to join and clearly directed to serious professionals (mostly stump speakers), wait until you've been through the Toastmasters and are into the local, learning talks. Then seek out a nearby chapter.

How much does it cost to use talks and speeches as a niche-selling means?

The costs come from researching your material, subsidizing your practicing, getting booked, and maintaining a support staff.

Researching your speeches is simply a part of learning more about your niche topic, then how to extract the key elements needed and packaging them into speech form. So it needn't be much beyond what you must pay anyway to become and maintain yourself as an expert in your niche field.

Since you aren't paid simply to talk, and getting there and the attendant expenses must come from your pocket, those must also be factored into the overall costs of eventually mastering this means. Often you will talk at gatherings of peers or others related to your niche topic. The ideal situation is where you learn more at the gathering, in value, than you pay to attend — plus you get to speak and display your expertise.

"Getting booked" is the hard part. It's often said in N.S.A. that 90% of your time and effort is spent getting that 10% booking. You do that yourself or let a speakers' or lecture bureau book you. Mike Frank, former president of the National Speakers Association and himself a speaker and bureau director, said "95% of our (speaking business) will come from our own marketing effort," in *Speaking for Money*, a book he and I coauthored.

That is, you find and directly contact the meeting planners, send the necessary selling tools (opening letter, brochure, fact sheets, audio or video demo tapes, testimonial letters) when needed, negotiate a date and fee, prepare, make travel arrangements, speak, and follow up. Every step costs. Brochures can be hundreds of dollars; a video tape, thousands. And a support staff

— sparse at the start but larger as needed — adds new dimensions: an office, furniture, insurance, perks.

How much does it cost? It can cost $5,000-100,000 a year to get yourself in front of eager listeners. Lest that scare you, if done wisely you will be earning three to four times more in return. The trick is to keep the income ahead of the outgo.

Some first-rate books will help you. The two best that cover the field completely are by Dottie and Lillet Walters, *Speak and Grow Rich* ($12.95/Prentice Hall), and Margaret Bedrosian, *Speak Like a Pro* ($14.95/John Wiley and Sons). Also particularly good is a book addressing the seven steps that lead to a super speech, by Art Fettig: *How to Hold an Audience in the Hollow of Your Hand* ($9.95/Growth Unlimited).

They also explain how to find and work with bureaus, who at best will be supplementary to your own marketing. Bureaus normally charge (keep) about 25% of the fee collected. You usually need a track record, brochure, demo tapes, and proven earning power before they will consider you. Even then you want to be selective about the bureaus you have represent you.

How does all of that affect niche marketing speakers? It depends upon the niche and how often it uses speakers, if and what it pays, and how much you wish to pursue this means, assuming you have or will develop the gift (the less gifted call it the art) of speaking.

My sense is that most niche marketers will hover between the talking and early speaking stage if they limit themselves solely to one topic in one field. Thus, wisely approached, their expenses will be low: they will be booked because of their unique knowledge and the fact they have spoken where others in the niche field have heard them. So they can probably avoid the cost of high-priced, multicolored brochures and three-camera video demo tapes.

But they can't avoid the need to master the craft and to produce a well designed and presented speech, since that will be the element that will project them upward as able, knowledgeable experts.

Some may find in their niche presentations a theme that they wish to develop and present to larger audiences. The degree to which they are successful doing that will be directly related to how well they play the bigger game: better selling tools, more sellers, bigger fees to pay for it.

How are talks and speeches best integrated with other means?

It works both ways. Niche buyers can want to hear you speak because they read what you said in an article, enjoyed your book, heard or saw your tapes... They perceive you as a person who has something to say, so they will listen. Which puts a huge burden on you if you're new to the speaking game. They expect you to be as good in that medium as you are in others. They expect a well crafted talk well delivered, informative and entertaining. Anything less and they will be disappointed.

Or it can happen in reverse. They hear you first, like what you say, want more good stuff from you, and seek other ways to share your message and, hopefully, your enthusiasm and inspiration.

Another good way to expand your speaking is to offer essentially (or even exactly) what you said on audiocassette, so buyers can hear you again at their own leisure. Or to take the theme and create a series of audiocassettes that will expand upon it.

If you are showing your niche market a new way to finish and stain a table or hide mole decapitators in the ground you might consider video rather than audiocassettes.

You can also sell your market a book, an anthology of articles, reports, a newsletter — any of the other means we address in this book.

Any final thoughts about talks or speeches as niche marketing tools?

Expanding upon that last segment and reiterating what I have said repeatedly, you must speak at as professional a level as you perform the other means that bring niche marketing attention to you. Experts are poorly received in areas where they are markedly wanting in competence.

If you are known because of your revelations made in a book and are comfortable in the arms-length milieu of writing but you are painfully uncomfortable, or incapable, of speaking well, then you would be wise to avoid direct speaking as a means of expanding the marketing of your expertise.

There is nothing shameful about being unable — or unwilling — to master and display all of the presentation crafts before a niche market. Better to do one excellently than others adequately or poorly.

But if you enjoy speaking, like the power of having a group ardently anticipating your every word, are thrilled by the clamorous cacophony of mesmerized nichers, and think you can help them at least as well orally as by other means, speaking is the path.

Or seminaring, as we'll see next.

Chapter 14B

Seminars

My sense is that most niche marketers who use speaking as a principal way to share and sell their core of unique information will seldom if ever stand before a throng of thousands, or even hundreds, microphone in hand, notes gone, looking into the eyes of an enraptured audience straining to hear that next revelatory spark.

Instead, they will give seminars (or workshops, training programs, etc.). Less electric, certainly less dramatic, but meatier, more substantial, trading flair and the masque for well ordered matter to be written down and read again later, then used and reused. Information delivered carefully, at rewriting speed, likely from notes — some flair permitted.

Speeches invite careful attention and claps of understanding and approval. But their very structure militates against depth. The rule of thumb: an eye-opener, three points, and an upbeat close. Speeches wave flags; herald new thoughts or processes; paint visual word pictures. There's too little time to dig in, to go beyond verbally sketched illustrations.

A good seminar digs, fills in, develops points through examples that are followed from creation to conclusion. It combines narration with workbook demonstration. And the logical form of listener response is a nod of gratitude, a sigh at having wrestled a concept to comprehension, an itch to give it a try. Note-taking hands are too weary for thumping applause.

Are seminars a good "lead" means for niche marketing?

You bet. They rank with books as the very best way to prove to a niche market that you know something well enough to explain it in depth. In this case you are willing and able to answer the questions that explanation or the topic provokes, you are articulate, and, even better, you are accessible. The people you want to reach can see and hear you. There is an immediate human link.

Your listeners will know after an hour or many whether you are an information leader worth following. Baptism by fire. So you don't want to offer a seminar until you are in fact ready to perform at the highest level and you have your information clearly thought through and in order. Let's talk more here about performance and the information being discussed.

To offer a memorable seminar you need to combine the theatrics of a performer and the didactic solidity of a professor.

Theatrics to the degree that the presentation is vigorous, energetic, seamless, and fast-moving. You must be fully present and involved; you must clearly want your listeners to understand what you are saying and feel the passion you have for your topic. All unstated: that must simply buttress and empower everything you do and say at the presentation.

Solidity in the sense of balance and strength. The seminar must have a goal, a clearly defined path to reach it, a leader who will guide the listeners along that path so that at every step they are understandably on course, and — usually — a map to tie the experiential to the mind and memory (all the better to mentally retake the trip in the future).

Therefore you must devise the goal and path, and find the best words to tell your listeners what is happening at the session. You are the leader; the map is the tools you will use to add to your words: slides, board writing, overhead projections, a film or video, perhaps a workbook, or many of those.

In my books about writing and publishing — particularly *How to Sell More Than 75% of Your Freelance Writing* and *Self-Publishing to Tightly-Targeted Markets* — I offer a simple organizational technique that is worth briefly repeating here, even though it will work as well for almost all of the information dissemination means. It suggests defining and organizing your seminar by (1) a purpose statement, (2) a working question, and (3) secondary questions.

Since you know your niche market and the core topic you wish to share with it, ask, "In one sentence, what is the purpose of this seminar?" That sentence is the purpose statement. Let's say that your specializations are both reading and gerontology. You decide that "the purpose of my seminar is to enhance grandparents' storytelling skills."

Convert that into a question. "How can grandparents become super storytellers?" The seminar then becomes the answer to that working question. That is the purpose and goal of the seminar, and anything that doesn't directly help achieve that purpose is excluded.

The secondary questions come from defining the working question and are usually preceded by one of the interrogatory words who, what, why, where, when, or how. Simply list any secondary question that comes to mind, like

> "Does 'grandparents' mean both grandfathers and grandmothers?"
>
> "Does it include older folks who are actually without grandchildren?"
>
> "Are younger adults excluded entirely?"
>
> "What is the purpose of becoming a super storyteller?"
>
> "Would the storytellers tell stories only to their grandchildren? Or to other children in schools? The library? In churches? Perhaps to the aged? Developmentally disabled?"
>
> "Would they be able to select stories that best fit their personalities? Or would they learn to adapt their personalities to the stories?"
>
> "Where would they find the best stories?"
>
> "Could they create their own stories? Or tell yarns tied to their own past? Or just ad lib?"
>
> "Might they integrate these stories with visuals shown on a VCR so they could be enjoyed by a large gathering?"

You might list 50 or even 100 secondary questions. Then go through the list and bunch like questions into categories. Finally, put the categories into a sensible outline, using the key questions as a guide for the kind of information and illustrations you will need to gather, and perhaps get or prepare, so that you can answer the working question fully and clearly within the time allotted.

Once you have a goal and path, you probably need ancillary teaching tools. Unless your information defies visual representation — an alien thought pattern might qualify — you would likely aid the listeners' learning by using slides or an overhead projector, writing on the board, or offering workbooks.

Whatever form you use, it must be done at the same level of professionalism that you wish to project to your niche market. Which means that the slides are sharp, clear, in order, rightside up, and have a purpose. The items to be projected on the overhead are large enough, uncluttered (unless the idea is to project clutter), and an asset to the verbal explanation. The board writing follows some order, is readable, and adds to the presentation. And that the workbooks visually portray the quality and cost of the seminar, are proofed error-free, significantly enhance the oral offering, aren't simply a written rendition of the words said, and will be intelligible and useful later.

And finally you must find the best words to guide your listeners — and the best skills to deliver them.

You know your niche market. Speak to be understood. If they use buzz words or jargon and those words are useful in explaining your information, then use them — but not to patronize. Mainly strive to clarify and share. Be yourself using your best English. You needn't buy new silver. Just dust off the best you have, line it up properly, and dig in. The value of your information, your enthusiasm, and the clarity of its organization will overwhelm the actual words used — if they are the right words for the right thoughts said in the right order, which is pretty much the way that most people speak when they have thought and planned first.

As for developing seminaring skills, there is no true practice field. Attend some seminars, see good presenters in action, then go to it. You will have a lectern to hold your notes, the words before you, and all your props at hand. Practice repeatedly until you feel comfortable, particularly the opening, closing, and key transitions. If you know your topic well, are fully present, and the presentation is well organized and scripted, speak.

What is the best way to use seminars for niche marketing?

The beauty of seminars is the speed with which they can be organized. A book takes months to write, prepare, and self-publish — years if it's being done by another publisher. Articles need months of lead time for major magazines. Newsletters, audiocassettes, and reports can be compiled more quickly but they are often second-strike means.

Yet a seminar can be given about as quickly as you can organize the contents, a workbook can be written and copied, and the nichefolk can be informed and gathered.

The state suddenly enacts a new regulation affecting llama herders. You are the expert. You create a plan that shows llama herders how to comply both quickly and inexpensively while significantly increasing their profits. You send a flyer to every herder in the state, announce that the seminar will be held at a certain location for "X" day; it will cost $195. That could be done within a month. A week if absolutely crucial.

Will they attend? Yep, if you're already the expert and they pay heed to your word. Probably, even if you're unknown, as long as that flyer fully outlines your qualifications or credentials, lists benefits they would receive that are greater than the cost and inconvenience of attending, and their need is sufficiently severe.

A related beauty to seminars: as quick as they are to organize and give, they are quicker to modify. If a seminar is already scheduled say a week off and new information appears in print that directly touches the participants, it can be instantly integrated and commented upon. Or if you wish to offer a follow up seminar expanding on material touched, or explaining new information just revealed, it is enough to announce that new seminar now, then bring the contents and workbook into existence by the date it is held!

So the best way to use seminars is as a lead means, particularly for new or changing in-depth material. But also as a place where you can display your other products and services, to be handled, prodded, leafed through, or smelled during the breaks, then bought in a frenzy at the end.

How profitable are seminars?

It depends upon how or where you offer them.

Sometimes you offer a seminar as part of a conference or convention. The organizers may pay you to do so: $100 honorarium (not much honor there) to several thousand dollars. Or they may give you the privilege of displaying your seminar intelligence, wit, and endowment free. In either case your take-home profits may be significantly bolstered if they also allow you to set up your own B.O.R. (back-of-the-room) product sales. If you have products (or can even get others' at discounted prices to sell), that could mean from $50 to many, many thousands of dollars more. (The highest B.O.R. income I ever heard of was $66,000 after a 150-minute motivation/inspiration seminar.) There are other considerations: will they pay your transportation, lodging, and board; will they pay your registration fee; must you pay to display; do they want a percentage of your product sale — and what will they give you in exchange (like the payments just mentioned and/or product sellers)?

Or your niche market can be reached through continuing education programs at colleges or universities. Which usually means that you schedule (and set aside dates on your calendar) about 120-180 days in advance, the seminar is included in a catalog or bulletin widely distributed locally, the school handles preregistration and provides a room or facilities, and you receive from 40-60% of the gross (sometimes net) income.

Which eliminates the "instant" programs to meet urgent needs. But it lets you pass the basic promotional and organizational work off to another group while you niche market in other ways, you prepare a workbook as the date approaches and if the preregistrations warrant it, and you simply show up that day, do your thing well, and reap the rewards. Payment through schools can run from $250-2,000 per program.

They also permit you to sell products after the session as long as that is completely secondary and does not in any way affect the seminar itself.

It varies little for other institutions, like hospitals and adult education.

When you offer seminars (or training sessions) through businesses or corporations, booking is the hard part. Finding the person closest to your niche-meeting needs requires the greatest diligence.

I suggest calling the company switchboard, telling the receptionist that you would like the name of or to speak with (the closest position to your niche market) about (skills training or the topic itself). If you want to follow this information with a letter introducing your program, its benefits for that company, and you as a specialist in the field, you want the person's name and exact position title. If you want to give this information orally, you want to speak to that person.

Any positive response will solicit something to review so they can consider bringing you in to offer your session. At that point you explain in writing, again, what the seminar is designed to do, why they would benefit, who you are to speak about it, any tools you use or items you leave (like workbooks or tapes), what other firms (with human names to call) have heard you give this program, and whatever else they request.

Should they hire you, the terms will be agreed to by contract or some form of binding agreement. You could receive from several hundred to several thousand dollars for the seminar. If the firm is more than 50 miles away they normally pay transportation and any necessary lodging and food. Plus any workbooks or like items left with the participants.

B.O.R. sales are inappropriate here but should you have, say, a book or a tape that would be of direct benefit to the seminar participant you might suggest to your booker a bulk sale for later distribution to the company's employees.

The riskiest form of seminar promotion is probably, after convention/conference booking, the most likely to be used by niche marketers: the self-sponsored seminar.

In it you absorb all of the costs. But you also get all of the profits — if there are any. We'll discuss those costs in response to the next question. But profits are possible — huge profits.

Since you already know your niche buyers and how to contact them, the greatest potential risk (of offering a general subject to a broad market and advertising by newspaper) is eliminated. You will send specific flyers to an interested market on a known mailing list.

Let's say your universe is 30,000. You plan to offer three seminars — one in the East, Midwest, and West. And you expect 200 to attend each, a full-day $149 program. That would bring in $89,400 from registrations. You also expect to sell a very modest $2,000 in products at each session, plus $1,000 more in resulting mail order. So that's $98,400 for a six days work, two days at each spot. Gross income, before the bills. But not bad — nor much out of line for niche marketing expectations.

The purpose of this book isn't to provide all of the operational details about each means but rather to put them into perspective from a niche marketing mode. My three-hour seminar tape series, with workbook, called "How to Set Up and Market Your Own Seminar," is extremely useful in filling in the how-to gaps, particularly about academic booking. (See details on the last page.) Also of specific interest is our report, "Generating Back-of-the-Room Sales."

How much does it cost to use seminars as a niche selling means?

The seminaring itself isn't expensive. A meeting room rental, some workbooks to be produced, getting to and from the site and survival costs while there. Those can easily be absorbed in the fee you charge. But what adds up, injects the risk, and must be paid in advance is the self-sponsored promotion just to get bodies to pay that fee and attend. The danger is obvious. You spend more attempting to fill the house than you gather through actual registrations!

So let's set aside the first three forms of seminars above. You know what you will earn at the convention or conference, plus product sales; you know by contract what the firm will pay you; and while you don't know what your cut of the percentage of the gate will be at the school programs until the gate stops swinging, you know that there will be no losses.

How much is it going to cost you to generate that $98,400 from three sessions, 200 at each paying $149 apiece, plus $9,000 in product sales?

If most of the products are yours (50-60% profit), the rest others' (35-45% profit); you bring them with you on the airplane (no additional freight), and the mail order buyers pay the shipping and tax (where required), you should earn about $4,500 profit — or half of the $9,000.

Assuming you live near one of the seminar sites, figure $1,000 for air fare for the other two, plus four nights at the other hotels at $100 each. Food, local travel, tips, incidentals at

$100/day away and $50/locally. And parking, $35 total. Total: $1,935.

Add to that $2.50 a workbook, or $1,500. Other paperwork: registration forms, evaluations, order forms, etc., $125. And temporary help selling products at all three sites: $300. Meeting room rentals at each hotel run $250, and since lunch is not included, other fees would be coffee and soft drinks, another $250 per site. Total: $3,425 more.

Promotion costs 45 cents a flyer, which includes printing, folding, mailing list rental and label application, mailing house fees, and bulk rate mailing. To 30,000 people that costs $13,500. Plus $1,000 to prepare the flyer itself and $3,500 overhead, including phone responses, employee time/costs, credit card fees, bank charges, and incidentals. Total: $18,000.

So you take the $98,400, subtract the $4,500 for products and $23,360 for the costs above, and you have a profit of $70,540. Not bad. Could you spare a dime?

Yet if you drew only 100 per session that profit would have drastically dropped. Figuring the gross income at $49,200 (cutting the product sales and workbook/paperwork costs in half and the total meeting room rentals and beverage costs to $450 each) and the total costs at $24,198, the profit would be $25,002. Still not too bad. A nickel?

But there is a point where self-sponsored seminars aren't worth the time and risk. In this case it's at about 50 per session, where the profits (again reducing some costs proportionately) would be $2,083. Not worth considering.

The problem remains, particularly when you are new to your niche field and don't have a proven sense of the mailing list's accuracy and drawing power: how many buyers will respond to your seminar, complete and submit the registration form with payment, travel elsewhere, endure strange bedding and food, buy their own lunch, and suffer (as only they can imagine suffering) just to hear you save their hide, fill their dreams, or give them a verbal boot in the butt?

Not included above is the bite that all of this planning, traveling, and talking does to you, your spirit, and your attention to other forms of niche marketing and to life in general. That's the sacrifice you make, of course — but there's a point, at least measured in profit, below which the candle is too heavy for the light.

How are seminars best integrated with other means?

The most immediate way is to make the same information and the same workbook available on audiocassette to those unable to attend the seminar that you are offering. Make it available some days later (say 10) and at a slightly higher price. This gives them the option of seeing and hearing you in person or gleaning the information, after the paying participants, at their leisure.

As mentioned, seminars provide an excellent opportunity to display your other products, even to discuss one or two of the most relevant during the presentation itself. The biggest sellers are usually books, reports, and audiocassettes, in that order.

Two kinds of requests most often come from well given seminars: consulting time and whether you are available to speak to groups, companies, or organizations.

In fact, for those not planning to pursue paid speaking as a primary marketing approach, this is an ideal way to back into smaller speeches, earn and gain experience, and test that means for future expansion. You can often get hired without a brochure or even demo tapes if the person hearing you at the seminar has sufficient clout — or the sponsor has sufficient need and courage!

Consulting is the most sought spinoff, though. Prospective buyers have seen you in person wrestling with facts, ideas, and concepts. They think you can solve a problem they have. So you ask some opening questions, and if you too believe that you can be of assistance the only thing left to resolve is the time, fee, and location.

Any final thoughts about seminars as niche marketing tools?

Seminars are my favorite for one reason: you make your impact in just three or four hours. You're able to show human dimensions — humor, compassion, the fact that you were where the listeners are at one time in your career, concern, love — that aren't evident by other means. From that comes a bonding with your audience that makes it easier for you to help them and for them to seek your guidance.

And seminars can be profitable, which you can then spread into developing your product roll-out by the other, initially less productive means.

Finally, there is no faster way to prove that you is or ain't an expert in one sitting. If you are, it's the jugular; if you're not, the noose.

"In America only the successful writer is important, in France all writers are important, in England no writer is important, and in Australia you have to explain what a writer is."

Geoffrey Cottrell, *New York Journal-American* (1961)

"In a very real sense, the writer writes in order to teach himself, to understand himself, to satisfy himself; the publishing of his ideas, though it brings gratifications, is a curious anticlimax."

Alfred Kazin, *Think* (1963)

Chapter 14C

Audio and Video Tapes

In this chapter I discuss audio and videocassettes prepared to impart information rather than those designed to entertain, like movies or music. Which is not to say that some elements of entertainment don't creep, or bound, into the information format, intentional or not.

Most of what I will say will be directed to speakers and entrepreneurs of the oral arts. Writers can also sell information orally — for example, we currently offer four tape series and two singles about writing-related subjects — but one markets tapes to written-word-oriented buyers at peril. Which is another way of saying that niche markets tend to be either written-word- or spoken-word-oriented.

Tapes are much more sought by the latter. Speech hearers and seminar participants are far more eager to buy something said or to be seen rather than written by a particular person they heard or saw before. Tapes are an ideal means to do that: they can be stored, played when the listener wishes, and heard or seen again and again in whole or part. They can even be duplicated and shared — to the seller's chagrin.

What is the best way to use tapes for niche marketing?

People can listen to audiocassettes almost anywhere now: in public with a Walkman, in the car, at the office. They are small and nearly indestructible inside their poly or Norelco boxes. The players are likewise small, portable, and usable virtually anywhere with batteries (and a headset). And they are inexpensive.

The typical starting price for a single information tape is $9.95 for 60 minutes; for a series, $9.95 times the number of tapes in the series plus $5-10 more for a workbook and holder (or $39.95 and up for a three-hour, three-tape series with workbook).

Who buys audiocassettes? Professionals (usually to listen to while commuting to work, at the airport, or on the airplane), salesfolk (to hear when driving on their rounds), self-improvement buffs (who are instructed, inspired, or warned by tape), and those who need to know specific information and find, for whatever reason, listening their mode of preference.

For your own niche marketing you should know how audiocassettes can help you sell your presentation skills. Speakers need audio demo tapes as part of their marketing kit. Rarely will an agency or meeting planner book you without having heard you speak, at least on tape. The same is true to a lesser degree for booking seminars through other sponsors. Colleges are less insistent; business, much more.

Those tapes are generally one of two kinds: (1) either the full seminar or speech, or a significant, uninterrupted part of it, or (2) snips and samples of one or many presentations included to show, for example, how you open, use humor, make a serious point through a story, invoke rending pathos or sundering sadness in the audience, and how you close to thunderous ovation. Often another voice introduces you, telling of your many accomplishments (chosen from hundreds to suit the booking audience) and what the listener is about to hear. Music sometimes wafts in and out, that other voice might summarize, and occasionally testimonials (in the praiser's own voice) follow the summary — or appear on the reverse side, with a reference to the testimonials made on the front. Demo tapes might be as short as 12 minutes or as long as a seminar or speech lasts.

Instructional videocassettes aren't so portable, popular, or inexpensive. And they cost you a ton to make, as we'll read in a subsequent section.

While they have fortunately become standardized into one playing format with the commercial demise of Beta, a VCR is still required to see them, which confines their viewing pretty much to the home or office.

Yet they are superb disseminators where seeing is learning: how to finish a dresser, how to safely slide into home, how to properly package prunes for portage in Papago. So if your niche market needs to know something that is simply better explained visually than written, videos must be seriously considered for your product or instruction arsenal. That, in turn, defines who buys videocassettes. Those who care enough to see something will pay to do so. The reward must be worth as much or more than the cost and the hassle.

When do you need videocassettes to sell your niche marketing skills? When you want to get paid to give speeches, and sometimes seminars. Audiocassettes and paper info sheets used to be enough to get booked at almost any level. Today, many speakers' bureaus and agencies will refuse to represent you without a video; others feel that without them you won't be booked for speeches or work above about $2,500. Meeting planners respond the same way. Why? Because they have been burned by poor speakers with slick packets. And because those who want to work at higher paying levels and have the skills also have professional video demos, along with or instead of audio demos.

How profitable are tapes? And what do they cost to produce?

Exact figures applicable to every kind of niche market are hard to determine because the conditions, markets, tape prices, and buyers are so varied. But one thing is certain: if you have a market that will buy tapes regularly or in quantity, the profits can be enormous.

Let's address audiocassettes first. If a 60-minute tape sells for $9.95, it will cost you less than a dollar to duplicate it if done in quantities of about 500 or more, about $1.85 if done in lots of 25+. Add to that from a dime to a quarter for each label (one for each side per tape) and another dime for the Norelco box (like those holding the master tapes you buy.) The alternative, poly boxes, which look cheaper but scratch less, are often provided free with each duplicated tape; at most they cost a few cents.

For audiocassette series you must add tape holders. These cost from $1.85-$4 each per three-tape or four-tape plastic pre-formed holder with a clear front plastic cover. Into that goes a printed insert label that can cost from 15 cents to several dollars, depending upon the number of colors and artistry. Or the holder can be silk-screened into hundreds of exquisite designs, which may cost from $2-4.50 each — far less in large quantity. If a workbook is also required, that may cost from $1-10, with perhaps a dollar added for a larger holder with a workbook well.

All that's left, whether it's a single tape or a series, is the cost of preparing a script (assuming you already know the information you wish to share); the cost of a tape deck, microphone with a stationary holder, amplifier and speaker, and master tape; or the rental fee for a studio (with the necessary equipment) and the engineer's fee; any editing expenses, and other incidentals like mailing.

Our in-house recording/amplifying equipment cost about $250 total at Radio Shack and took a while to learn to use well but has never failed us even though I haul half of it on tour much of the year. Better equipment is available for about the same price today.

Full-service studio rental fees in the greater Los Angeles area run about $50 an hour, which includes the engineer, all equipment, and editing. (Newcomers should generally calculate four times the length of the final recorded tape for total studio time, or four hours for a C-60, or one-hour, tape. You may not actually be at the studio that many minutes; the difference would be the engineer's editing, which can be done with you in attendance or not.) A range for studio fees nationwide might be from $20-85.

If music is included, figure about $35 for royalties for each piece chosen. (Many tapes will have parts of the same piece at the opening and closing.) Other sound bytes — car backfiring, mime bellowing, laughter, applause — are usually inserted free. If you need an outside narrator, studios have sample demo tapes with vying narrators' names and phone numbers. You make your own arrangement with the person selected, who comes to the studio at the recording hour and narrates according to your script — you hope. Fees run from $30-150 an hour.

The first tapes pay off the equipment or studio time plus the script preparation. After that you can expect a 60-70% profit ratio on every tape sold. Budget from less than a hundred dollars per tape, if you have equipment, to about $1,250. (A friend just spent $1,200 for 250 C-60's totally produced by a professional house, including original music, a narrator, a "J" card, impressed labels, and individual shrinkwrapping; to reorder it will cost $189 for another 250 of the same tapes.)

A king-sized bonus: you can order your tapes in quantities of 25 or 50, when needed. That ties up a minimum amount of money in inventory, uses little shelf space, and lets you change your audiocassettes as often as necessary to keep up with the changing demands of your niche buyers.

Videocassettes require roughly the same production components but they cost much more to produce. Thus they are a greater profit-loss risk, require more up-front capital, and must be thought through much more carefully before you branch into their arena for market products.

You can save a significant hunk of cash by producing the essential video footage with a home camera, good film, sufficient lighting, complementary background, and a clear audio. You can also build your own tank given the right parts and instructions. One is about as sensible as the other, particularly if this video is to show you as a professional imparting important information. Or it is to convince another booker that you should be hired to speak about your field of expertise.

The three most important components are (1) something worth putting on video, (2) excellent video footage, and (3) professional editing. The rest — duplication, labels, boxing, and so on — are done about the same way for videocassettes as they are for audiocassettes, often by the same companies.

Presumably what you want to video is best shared by that medium, you or the others you employ to speak and act can convey that information clearly and with at least a modicum of flair, and you can produce a script that details the text and movement. See first what else is being shown your target market, then do it one (or several) better.

At that point shop around — friends, *Yellow Pages*, other speaking professionals — and find several nearby videotape producers. Explain what you have in mind, let them suggest ways to realize that, costs, and time factors. Take what several say, create a plan, and hire the one who you think will do the best job for you and that you can afford.

Generally that producer will provide at least two cameras, with operators, to photograph you performing before a live audience (does anybody perform before a dead audience?) or in studio, probably adding audience noise, laughter, and applause. Depending upon the length of the presentation, distance to travel, and related concerns, that can cost from $150 to several or many thousand.

Then the film must be edited. If you are giving a 60-minute talk, you may want one of three kinds of editing: (1) a full presentation with just the gaffs and goofs snipped and blended, so it can be sold as a product, (2) a 6- to 12-minute demo video, severely pruned to show you at your best, or (3) the demo first and the full program last, on the same tape, with a bridge explanation that "if the viewer is interested, the full program follows from which the demonstration just viewed was taken."

Editing can cost anywhere from several hundred to several thousand dollars, and usually exceeds the initial shooting costs. It can be done either by the video producer or at the duplication studio, if you submit unedited film to them to produce a clean, final product. From either you receive a master video.

From the master, duplicates are produced. Sample costs might be as follows: 20-minute video, 50 = $4.80 each; 100 = $4.25; 250 = $3.50; 500 = $3.25. And for a full hour, 50 =$5.75; 100 = $5.25; 250 = $5.10; 500 = $4.75. One-color labels are either included or must be added at 10-25 cents each, two per cassette.

Videocassette albums or holders come in solid color or transparent models and hover around $2 each, with the range from about $1.75-$5. Other than the clear holders, most have see-through traps unsealed at the spines into which you can insert a full, wraparound label. Those can cost from 15 cents to several dollars depending upon the artwork and intricacy.

If the video is directed at speakers' bureaus and meeting planners, you may wish to have testimonials edited into the text, probably at the end. These can be shot with less skill on a hand-held home video camera, by you or friends.

The global costs for a video? Probably from $750 to $2,500, and one hears of videos produced for as low as $200 to as high as $5,000. The length of the tape figures far less in the cost than the quality of filming and editing.

Are they profitable? If they are used as products, since one can charge from $29.95 to several hundred dollars each, yes, if bought in sufficient quantity they can be a true windfall, since, like audiocassettes, you can order small duplication quantities as needed.

If they are used as tools to get you booked, they are profitable to the degree that they secure bookings. Awful videos don't engender bookings and cost the same as terrific videos. So if you need videos, pay the price, make them terrific, then talk up a storm to your niche buyers!

Are tapes a good "lead" means for niche marketing?

It simply depends upon your topic and your market.

They can be where your niche buyers want to see or hear the information you are sharing. But usually people want something they can easily return to, like a fact written in an article or book, and they want some human interplay with the speaker, such as they get in a seminar.

Once you have established that human touch, even if it's as remote as their listening to your speech, and have provided the factual base they can touch back to for depth, then tapes are ideal second-level means for expanding upon a point or extending a mood or inspiration.

How are tapes best integrated with other means?

One way is obvious. If you offer a seminar about a key subject that has many offshoots that also beg to be discussed in depth, you can either offer additional seminars about the offshoots, you can produce a tape about them, or you can do both.

Let me give you a current example. My seminar "How to Sell 75% of Your Freelance Writing" walks one through the process of selling, then writing articles for magazines and newspapers, and includes a short segment about converting those articles into books. Many of the elements discussed during that four-hour session lend themselves to far more discussion. One is "Research: Finding Facts, Quotes, and Anecdotes"; another, "Finding Ideas for Articles and Books That Sell." Yet if I dwell unduly long on those topics in the seminar, the balance is disturbed and other, critical elements aren't properly covered.

So I created 60-minute audio tapes about each of those subtopics, and sell them after the seminar to those needing more specific help at those points. (Alas, they are writers not comfortable with oral instruction. So I also took the tape scripts and reworked them into reports by the same title, so they could buy by either means. I also took the seminar script, expanded it considerably, and turned that into a written format as well: the book called *How to Sell More Than 75% of Your Freelance Writing.*)

Another area where cassettes are used to great benefit is in inspirational and motivational fields. Suzanne Vaughan radiates outward from Denver to speak to nurses, women's groups, and teenagers (14-18) about stress management and self-esteem. Whether she's talking about "The Courage to be Imperfect" or "There's Life after a 'D' in Calculus," she impassions her audience, imploring and empowering her listeners to action. But once she's gone, how do her listeners keep that excitement and conviction alive? By buying her 55-minute tape called "Believe in Yourself: the Stars are Within You!" to listen to when they need reaffirmation, support, and permission.

Any final thoughts about tapes as niche marketing tools?

The discussion above has been based on today's technology, which in turn affects the cost of the items and their usability by your niche market.

We are on the cusp of huge technological changes. CD-Interactives (discussed in the following section) will dramatically alter the video field while both digital compact cassettes and mini compact discs will replace audiocassettes soon and probably forever.

Does that mean that you should sit back and wait for the changes before you expand into tape creation for your niche markets?

Yes and no. Audiocassettes are relatively inexpensive, the equipment won't be thrown away if something new comes along, and the younger generation has developed a habit of listening to "music" that way, so modest audio tape investment should provide help and reap profits long before the items slide into 8-track limbo. Then when the changes come you simply switch your message into the new format.

I'd be more cautious regarding videocassettes for sale to your niche market, unless the demand and profit is clearly evident and the selling curve isn't too long. But if you need a video to sell your skills to others, mainly to promote your own speaking and get booked, you may have no choice but to do the video now and hope it can be integrated into the newer technology later.

Chapter 14D

Compact Discs,
CD-ROMs,
and
CD-Is

When you supply vital information to your niche market you must keep two things in mind. One, the information can be supplied by many means or formats. Which format is determined by the capacity of each (i.e., working through a project one-on-one calls for consulting and can't be done by an article), its cost, whether you can or wish to provide the information that way, and how the niche consumer prefers to buy it.

And two, there is a tendency to look at the newest, jazziest form of dissemination first, then look backward. Since the advent of video, how many people use their old home movie cameras?

Well, CD-Is (compact disc interactives) are the new flash on the block, and for some forms of niche marketing they are spectacular for they include almost every means of information dissemination we have discussed in this book intermixed and in action simultaneously — with the exception of the in-flesh advantage of talks, speeches, seminars, and consulting.

What's the difference between the three?

CDs mean compact discs, those marvelous 4 3/4" metallic platters used with compact disc players to produce music as rich and faithful as if the soundmaker were in the room. Their fidelity and near indestructibility comes from the fact that the sound is numerically encoded, in digital form, and thus can be stored and extracted (by laser) without deterioration.

CD-ROM is different. It is an information retrieval system for computers, and thus requires some knowledge of computer programs to create and operate. But it is also digital, rather than analog in form, and is true in fidelity and permanence. What gives CD-ROM a huge advantage over standard computer disks and CDs, which it resembles, is the massive amounts of information it can hold in a small space. And that it can combine that data with music, photos, and video — still and moving. But CD-ROM also requires special computer equipment to be accessed and used.

CD-Is are not computer-linked but are discs that look like CDs and are played on special CD-I players connected to television sets. Regular musical CDs, like the new photo CDs, can be played on a CD-I player, though it doesn't work in reverse.

What is unique about CD-Is? The range of their interactivity. Both the CD and CD-ROM are essentially passive media: they produce what is stored in the order it is called up. As with audio and videocassettes, there is a form of one-dimensional interactivity since you can start, stop, select, fast forward, reverse, search, and pause, but that is limited to the means at hand and on display.

With a CD-I, you hook the player to any television set, switch it on, insert a CD-I disc, start it up, and with your controller (which looks like a TV remote control switch) in hand, you are in command.

What you see on the television combines text, video, still pictures, sound (narration, music, and sound effects at CD quality), and graphics — all mixed in a true multimedia format. But if it stopped there it would simply equate television. With CD-Is you can make choices about what you want to see next.

For example, let's say there were a CD-I disc about the magnificent Iguaçú Falls that separate Brazil from Argentina a few miles south of the Paraguayan city of Ciudad del Este. The controller will give you options on how you visit that site. You may wish to take the shoreline trail walk in the national park near the Brazilian Hotel das Cataratas, to see most of the cascades facing you on the Argentine side. You could view them roaring vertically downward in front of you. Using an arrow on the screen you could look to the left or the right, or even behind you, each with the thundering backsound that sight would bring, from key "hot spots" on the trail. If a coati walked to the side of the path to look at you, you could zoom in closer to look at it.

If you wanted to know the facts about the falls, or their names (there are some 270 of them, many two-tiered, stretched over 2 1/2 miles), you could click that information on screen, or listen to it. If you simply wanted to see the ten largest falls there, you could see those in any order. Want to go to the foot of an elevator, lean over, and have the Floriano Falls break just overhead and a bit out of reach? You can explore every angle and view from that vantage point.

Perhaps you'd rather go to the Argentine side and peer over the falls themselves, from miles of wooden catwalks. You can do that by simply walking along the trail or by selecting the falls you wish to gaze over. Why not take a powerful motorboat into the frothing "Devil's Mouth," then disembark at San Martín Island and hike to the top of the same churning cascade? Want to see what the motorboat and the roaring waters look like from shore? Click again. Want to see the cliff that Robert de Niro climbed in "The Mission," first from the bottom, then half way up, then from the top looking down, and finally from a helicopter (which you can also ride on the disc)? Click away, in any order you wish.

What about the history of the falls? Yours to see in still photos. Want a graphic showing how the falls compare with the smaller Niagara — or others in the world? A look at the wildlife commonly seen in the surrounding national parks? Click.

This is a fictitious but faithful example of what other discs in existence do and show. There are just over 100 discs now available, costing about $40-50 each, but that will mushroom in the near future.

Such a breadth of interactivity can take place because the CD-I combines digital recording, computer memory (on the disc and accessed inside the CD-I player), and the sound and visual advances of today's technology, then displays them on a large television screen. CD-I players became available in the U.S. in October, 1991, and cost about $600. In early 1993 they can be bought at Sears, Montgomery Wards, Circuit City, Good Guys, Silo, and Radio Shack.

What is the best way to use these compact disc items for niche marketing?

My sense is that CDs will not move much beyond their current use for music, with the advent of inexpensively combining both the sound and visuals so close and that being so much more practical for niche marketing. So I am going to abandon discussing them (in marketing terms) at this point, as I relish CD sound in the background while writing this book!

CD-ROMs

CD-ROM has some very specific advantages and four key disadvantages. It can hold gargantuan amounts of readily accessible data — per disc, the equal to 350,000 typewritten pages or 330 floppy disks — that can be seen or read by many means.

But as yet the disk cannot be written on though it can be copied into the hard drive and integrated into your other copy. Once the information is burned onto the disk, that is it: no additions, no subtractions, no alterations.

In the beginning the optical drives needed to read the disks cost as much as $3,000; now they are in the $300 range (though another $400 more may be needed to make IBM-compatibles able to reproduce the music and sound). Some computers now come with optical drives installed.

Calling up the data was slow. That too has been remedied. It is about as quick now as reading floppy disks.

And there was a basic disc incompatibility between Macs, IBMs, and other lines. The MPC logo should guarantee a Multimedia PC standard, but it doesn't help those discs produced earlier.

Will the buyers in your niche market be able to use CD-ROMs? There may be 1.5 million drives in use today. In June, 1992, Alan Sund, CD-ROM marketing manager for Sony's U.S. subsidiary (which has 40% market share) told *Fortune* (in "CD-ROM: The Next PC Revolution," by Mark Alpert), "We've reached critical mass. There are enough CD-ROM drives out there now to make the market profitable."

How are CD-ROMs currently being used to meet niche needs? To show American Airlines customers, through travel agencies, hotels where they might stay (an outside view, the lobby, pool, rooms, and more). Ford car parts cataloged back to the 1980 model year and updated monthly through a new disc. The last 36 years of New York state law cases. Every residential telephone listing in the U.S., on two discs. Street-level maps of every square mile in the U.S. Basic information on all the 1990-91 patents (at a rate of 2,000 issued in an average week).

Or fast-find machinery in your local library, like the one where all of the initial research for this book was done. Plus the basic reference texts, like *Compton's Encyclopedia*, on CD-ROM, which bring not only words but much more. Want to know about baseball? Check a reference CD-ROM — it will tell you. Want to see and hear the Babe's goodbye speech? There it is. See a picture of Ty Cobb? Bingo. Know how to pronounce a certain word? It will pronounce it.

Where CD-ROM will play an expanding role is in business and in libraries, where television sets are impractical and the sharing of data is foremost. And for niche buyers who need lots of data that can be easily cross-referenced.

CD-Is

The best way to use CD-Is, if any at present because of the huge cost of preparation, is for sale to corporations or businesses. You can command from $1,000-5,000 (or more) for a full training video now. If it had the additional interactive capabilities, and there were enough discs bought, the cost:profit ratio for CD-Is might justify their serious consideration in that market.

In Tony Buck's well researched report, "A Publishers Intro. to CD-I," he sees the brightest future for CD-Is in the educational field, where the average product has a lifespan of 25 years and the technology budget is growing almost twice as fast as the textbook budget and is estimated to reach $2.2 billion in 1994. Used as learning tools, Buck sees the key advantages for adapting CD-I's in schools as reduced learning time, lower cost (technology is cheaper than people in the long run), quality (you can get the top experts in each field for the CD-Is), privacy (no embarrassment at asking questions), greater retention, fun, and the CD's usability on the same player.

When the costs drop, however, the potential uses for CD-I for virtually all niche markets are many. Introductory skills, sales techniques, multimedia conferencing with all related data and visuals at hand, catalogs, product displays (you could not only see motorboats, you could ride in each, compare the costs, look at the motor and structural parts in detail and depth), step-by-step instruction discs (with every sane question answered as you went along) for everything from meat cutting and spying to building a birdhouse. Yet it's too early now to seriously consider CD-Is for consumers. And very early indeed to consider them at all for anybody without very, very deep pockets.

How profitable are CD-ROMs and CD-Is, and how much do they cost to produce?

CD-ROMs

Profit is directly related to what the buyer will pay for the finished product. While there are 3,000+ CD-ROM discs now available, commercial items sell for less than $100 (often $50-80) and would have to be mass produced for sufficient returns.

Business discs, however, can command from several hundred to $2,000 apiece, and if the item is a repeater — a catalog regularly renewed or updated inventory reports — profit leaps!

As in CD-Is, as we shall see next, the actual reproduction of the CD-ROM costs far less than the original concept, design, and pulling together of the information on a hard disk, a one-off CD, or a cartridge. (The process is described in full, costed detail by Liza Weiman in "A Practical Guide to Publishing CD-ROMs" in the April 1992 issue of *Macworld*.)

Often a team is needed to create the basic product: interface designers, graphic designers, and programmers. The size and composition of the team is directly related to what your disc does, its complexity, how much direction the user will need, and how presentable the final product must be.

146

Sometimes it is little more than collecting the data on a large-capacity hard disk drive and sending that to a CD-ROM manufacturer, who can transfer the data and press the discs.

In her article, Liza Weiman compares seven CD-ROM manufacturers on the cost of premastering, mastering, disc replication/packaging, master storage/reorder charge, and one-off charges for 5001 CD-ROM discs. The low bid was $9,260; the high, $11,552, a spread of $2,292 and a cost of about $2 a disc for production.

So a CD-ROM is relatively easy and inexpensive to produce, harder and much costlier to create, and hardest of all to match to a niche market unless your expertise is data-linked or your buyer is well equipped to use multimedia data/instruction information with a CD-ROM base.

CD-Is

Profits are possible at present with CD-ROMs. That's doubtful with CD-Is as yet. The costs are so hefty that's where your attention must now be directed.

Let's again rely upon Tony Buck's report, where he sees the time guidelines and costs as follows:

	TIMELINES	PRODUCTION COSTS
Concept/Design	2-3 months	$25-30,000
Script/Programming	3-6 months	$70-250,000
Test/Final	1-3 months	$30-70,000
Total	6-12 months	$125-350,000

Contrasted to the massive production costs, the WORM (write once, read many) test discs cost only $300 each, the CD-I masters might cost $1500-2000 apiece, and the CD-I disc copies with packaging would cost but $1.40-7.50 each, depending upon the quality.

Buck calculates that it would take a sale of 20,000 disc copies at $40 retail each to be successful on a $300,000 investment for the consumer market.

While the costs are high, CD-I has some positive elements to commend it. Not only is there a world standard for the machine, it and the discs are affordable. Moreover, the discs are extremely difficult to alter and copy.

But there are limitations and areas of concern. CD-I discs now contain 650 megabytes of memory, which can be used for roughly 19 hours of speech; 7,000 high resolution pictures; 300,000 pages of text, and 72 minutes of partial screen full motion video — mixed as needed. But they can't at present be used to reproduce videocassettes of movies.

And there can be horrendous difficulties securing the rights to all of the media components, plus translations which must be incorporated at the production level.

You don't produce these yourself, of course. You locate many firms that are actively involved in CD-Is, discuss your project, and bid out your product. Buck's report contains a list of such firms and further production details ($15 cost: contact Tony Buck at P.O. Box 231, Narberth, PA 19072; (215) 667-1702) or you might contact the CD-I Association of North America, 11111 Santa Monica Blvd., #750, Los Angeles, CA 90025/(310) 444-6619.

Are CD-ROMs and CD-Is good "lead" means for niche marketing?

CD-ROMs, maybe — in the distant future. CD-Is, heavens no, unless you and I are playing with far different mental cards. They are much too expensive as a first product. Unless you know your market intimately, have a sensitive thumb on its spending pulse, and have a concept in mind that is truly interactive and will be gobbled up as fast as you can spin your CD-I discs out, they are the very last product to consider. Now.

But that will change, as all things in the technology world do. You want to keep the CD-I card in your deck, and review it regularly, nibbling with the partial formats in between: audio and videocassettes, the many text-sharing formats. Meantime, keep your information digitally-based so that if/when CD-Is become feasible, it is relatively simple to convert. Also, keep track of where things come from so when you need to secure rights, you can. (The best way to do that is to produce all of the components yourself. If you sell rights to others, keep the electronic rights separate and clearly demarcated for your own later use.)

Any final thoughts about compact disc items as niche marketing tools?

One short, one prophetic.

The short one is not to save up your money for one giant splash with a CD-I. Rather, zero in on your niche market's needs now and meet them by the means with which people are currently comfortable and for which they are equipped. Then as they move into the higher technological ranks, you do too.

Anyway, CD-Is are not a panacea, just the most exciting and all-inclusive instrumentality hitting the market today. They simply will not work, or come close, to meeting most of the niche marketing needs now. Oddly, the simplest means will probably still work best for the bulk of your niche marketing needs far into the future.

The vision of the prophecy coincides with what I see as the greatest change facing niche marketing, but the facts aren't mine. They come straight out of George Gilder's *Life After Television: The Coming Transformation of Media and American Life* (Whittle Direct Books, 1990).

Let me draw from Gilder and blend his thoughts into niche marketing now and in the future.

He begins by saying, "(T)he microchip will reshape not only the television and computer industries but also the telecommunications industry and all information services. It will transform business, education, and art. It can renew our entire culture. The downfall of television turns out to be only the most visible symbol of a series of cascading changes that will engulf the world in the 1990s."

The current fear of Japanese dominance in America's television future, with the development and mass importation of HDTVs, isn't the issue either for the public or us as niche marketers. Who cares if we can see sitcoms and American gladiators better on a sleek, thin model hanging like a picture on the wall?

The future is in fiber optics and the telecomputer. For starters, some veterans of Next and Apple, known as Frox, are working on a machine that will connect with CD-ROMs, edit out TV ads, program the VCR, search databases for selected new items, and answer the telephone. (If they could just get it to wash the dishes, dog, and rug.)

But that's just the beginning. When fiber optics reach every home, we will all be able to tap into virtually any digitalized information font — interactively. We will tell it what we want, when, and in what format. Once there exists a national integrated services digital network of fiber optics, we will be freed from the low-level, limited outlet offered by television as the primary shaper of American culture and education.

The idea is to limit the number of wires, embed the switches in the microchip in each phone, television, computer, fax machine, and database, and hook those to one continuous fiber-optic cable, thus shifting the intelligence — accessible at any time on the cable — from some remote network or data provision service to the customer.

A science fiction concoction as unlikely as flying people? One study says that the volume of data will double 19 times before the year 2000. The problem is getting to the particular kernel of data that you and your niche customers need.

Cryptologics has a way. Send the information on unused FM radio sidebands, direct a hand-held tuner to extract what you want, and *voilá*: what you need. According to Gilder, "Two sidebands of one FM station could transmit 100 million words of data a day, or about the content of 1,000 full-length books. This would be like transmitting almost one book every minute and a half all day long and searching them for key words: a rate that is well within the capacity of current microelectronic scanners."

How would telecomputers change our lives? It will make home schooling feasible and attractive, with the best teachers in America a cable's length away. Key people will work at home, in touch through a global fiber network with their boss, the marketing director, or an overseas colleague (all life-size on high-definition video) and a button's distance from almost instantly retrievable documentation.

One could travel in the living room to any spot in the world through high-resolution screens. Want to see a movie? Call it up on the video selector and fix your own popcorn at about a quarter a big box! A concert? It's at hand. Read a book, calculate 6.7% compound interest over nine years, locate specific references to Machado de Assis translated from Portuguese, see how deep you should plant rose bushes, find out if the snow base is sufficient for skiing at a Chilean resort? It's all there to be accessed.

Niche marketing? Gigitons of data are just so much data until somebody pulls them together and applies them to needs at hand. Fiber-optics is a means of conveyance, not a mind capable of taking data, life, experience, need, motivation, profit, time, energy, and process and making it useful to others, and hence a product to sell.

What these breathtaking changes mean is that some time soon what you sell may have to be provided and packaged differently. It may be more or less valuable. Rather than the facts, you may in fact be selling the means by which those readily accessible facts are employed. Your selling slant may turn upside down. But the basic concept of niche marketing won't change a whit: find something that others desperately need, package it, and sell it.

And in the meantime, while we wait for our world to spin into some new techno-orbit, write articles and books, publish reports, consult, speak, and keep everything you can digital!

"In a certain sense, printing proved a draw-back to letters. It ... cast contempt on books that failed to find a publisher."

Remy de Gourmont (1858-1915)

Chapter 14E

Consulting

There are many forms of consulting, so we should perhaps discuss those first before we try to stuff the means into a niche-serving mold.

Consult means confer, advise, ask for assistance or direction, counsel. Somebody pays you for your expertise, experience, knowledge, wisdom, thought — plus time and presence.

One way of defining consulting is by time. An emergency occurs; they call and need instant advice. A long-range plan is being formulated; they need outside help to design the project, oversee its implementation, test its effectiveness, and provide ongoing feedback during its first months or years.

Presence is another element. They want you "on call" for spot or instant telephone help. They want a two-hour guidance session at their office or yours. They want you to live on-site for five days to review the operations. They want you to review the blueprint, sent to your office by Fedex, and to return any modifications by FAX.

You are normally paid by the hour or, having reached a previous understanding, by the project or by some longer time period, like a day, week, or month. The shorter the contract, the higher the per/hour rate. Confidentiality is generally understood as existing between you and the client — sometimes to the point of having to use proprietary material sight-only at their locale.

Paying related expenses generally follows the path used for speeches. If the costs are incidental or the commute is short, it is absorbed in the rate. But significant costs are added to the hourly or project rate, usually on a per-item basis, sometimes with a per diem included.

What is the best way to use consulting for niche marketing?

It happens the other way around. You are brought in for consultation because you are knowledgeable about the niche field. That is, you don't hang up a shingle as a consultant in a particular field if you are brand new to it, unknown in the area, or have yet to display any signs of having some experience, wisdom, or knowledge to sell.

Usually the person requesting your services has somehow been drawn to you and has made a judgment about your expertise. They have read an article or book you wrote (or that praised you); they heard you give a talk, speech, or seminar, or they were directed to you by somebody else whom they respect that knows you or of you, usually by one of those ways.

But that's not to say that, once you decide to consult in a field, you simply wait to be discovered. You do indeed "hang up your shingle": run ads in the appropriate journals, send printed matter to those most likely to pay for your services, network with those needing your help, let fellow consultants know that you are available should they have an overage or need assistance, plus crank out more articles, tapes, reports, and other signals that you have information for let or sale.

How profitable is consulting?

It depends upon how much you charge and how often you consult.

Rates run from about $25 an hour to many hundreds, with perhaps $75-135 a typical range. Let's say you charge $100/hour. Then you'd probably charge $600 or $650 a day (of eight hours), perhaps $2,500-2,750 a week (of five eight-hour days), and maybe $8,500-10,000 a month.

You might also have variable rates. I know of a book editor in the engineering field who charges $100/hour when discussing book production but will read, edit, and rewrite text if it's computer-accessible for $40/hour — if it can be done in his" off" time, which means he wants an extra week to get it back to the client.

When you're not busy or looking for a change of pace from writing and speaking, a few hours or days of consulting can be "found gold." A surprise blessing: a call, a problem to solve, a check, and back to work. But when you are busy and a good client "just needs a couple of hours," it can be a grind made no less bearable by the payment, which in that case will probably be delayed!

How much does it cost to use consulting as a niche selling means?

Other than advertising, which you may never do beyond adding consulting to the list of your services, what costs would you have?

You either have an office or you work out of your home, so you have a place to meet clients if they prefer to come to you. (You can also meet in neutral territory: a restaurant, a conference room in the library, the park.)

You have a phone, perhaps a FAX and modem. You have a car to get to them.

What you are selling is in your head, aided by a hearty handshake and a smile. All free. Consulting is the art of cashing in one very dull book and long night; on tinkering, fooling around, trying this and that; on learning the basics, then trying to fit them into new molds; on gathering every tidbit and key fact, old way and new process; on putting all you know and have done, read, seen, and heard into one particular situation or problem now. The pay is almost an embarrassment.

Is consulting a good "lead" means for niche marketing?

No. It comes from proving yourself by other means. There might be exceptions. If you just popped down from Venus and others want to know what Venusians would buy, drive, read, or wear, you have two choices: babble free or babble for bucks (consult). The rest of us will have trouble "leading" with consulting.

How is consulting best integrated with other means?

Usually it is your sharing by other means that brought you the consulting in the first place.

If you have a variety of products and services of use to buyers in your niche field, that puts you in an odd situation. Your obligation in consulting is to provide the best, unbiased information and advice possible. Often that includes suggesting that they avail themselves of more information by many means.

I often provide an annotated reference list on which my products and others are listed in order. If my product is the best, it goes first. If not (rarely, as you can imagine), another item goes first. No conflict.

Another way to make your related services known is, at the end of the consulting session, simply give the other person a list of your products and services and say that should any of these be of interest by their firm in the future, please let you know. You will probably follow up your consulting session with a checkup phone call several days or a week later. They may ask about your products or services then. If they don't, let a month or so go by, then you are free to more aggressively market yourself to them by other means.

Any final thoughts about consulting as niche marketing tools?

In the niche marketing field consulting is the reward for having positioned yourself right, convinced somebody that you know something worth paying to hear (or read), and made yourself available.

It's logical that successful practitioners often retire, then make more money than they earned before by consulting about the very thing they did earlier! People will pay for knowledge. If you have some core element of knowledge to sell, they want to buy, and they know how to find you, great! They usually know how to find you because you made it obvious that you were the person to hire by sharing parts of that information by other means.

It wasn't coincidental that when I listed the niche marketing means in this book I put consulting last. It really can be a pot of gold at the end of the rainbow.

Chapter 15

Awful Writers and True Mumblers
Are Also Invited

Paradoxically, you needn't know much about writing or speaking at all to cash in on this kind of niche marketing. In fact, you could succeed and be both illiterate and dumb, in the literal sense.

There are others, gifted, who can help you take up the communication slack.

That's because you're not selling communicative skills *per se*. Your market is buying the information that you are writing or speaking about. The information itself, and what it does or leads to.

What you can't be is too dumb in the other, "lack of intelligence" sense, at least as it pertains to identifying both a core topic and a target market, then selling it something vital.

WRITING

An ideal scenario would have you dazzlingly endowed with ideas, perception, marketing acumen, and literary ingenuity. Sometimes such souls do flash onto the scene — you hope in another field entirely.

But most of us are more drably festooned: we have what seems to us to be a good idea, a suspicion that others would pay to learn more about it, a sense of how to reach them — but no idea if we should write or say "farther" or "further."

Which is almost always enough because it's that idea and the information behind, around, and in front of it that we are selling — faster and more profitably if we know who and where its buyers are. We can probably overcome our commonplace communication skills as long as we can express our idea at least well enough for another person to decipher and clearly explain it.

Blessedly, there are such people who excel at taking vague concepts and flabby thoughts and converting them into pristine, rapier prose from which articles, books, reports, newsletters, and most of the speaking scripts are produced.

The kind of writing helper you need depends upon the level of thinking and writing skills you possess. (That level, incidentally, isn't static. It rises with close observation, analytical reading, maturity, sobriety, and practice.)

If you can barely get starter words on paper or tape, you need a perceptive ghost writer. They are often expensive and hard to find. Ghosts usually demand a hefty advance (several thousand to $10,000+ is common) plus a percentage of the royalties, often 50. They will produce a final draft from your ramblings; getting that draft published is up to you.

Most newcomers to niche marketing, however, begin their careers at the rewriter plateau. They can put the information down in about a B- fashion. Clear enough to be understood but hardly the stuff to make others, lumbering through the turgidity, want to rush to the phone to order more, much less mentally certify the writer as an "expert" on anything.

If you are at this level what you need is a wordsmith, a clever soul who can transform muddled thinking and arduous composition into surefooted, fast prose that states clearly, fires the proper images, and leaves the impression that you, the writer, have full command of the topic and know how to share it. You need a magician who can turn the task of reading your revelations into a learning delight.

Rewriters are more abundant and cost far less than ghosts, if you give them a solid base from which to work. They will take your words and do with them what you want: presumably, read clearly and convey the message fully to your targeted audience. Anything more, you must tell the rewriter before he/she begins. That might include the mood or speed of the piece, any image you wish it to provoke, other information you want inserted, its length.... The more you add, the more difficult it is for the rewriter to do, the longer that takes, and the more it costs.

Rates for rewriters, if hourly, run from about $12-75. Most prefer to work on a job basis, stating a set fee for an initial consultation and rewrite, your review, and any final touching up. If you and the rewriter are using compatible software, the work can often be done even faster and less expensively.

You may be so skilled at writing that ghosts or rewriters aren't necessary. That means that your writing is as good as what you read in your field, and with attention you could make it better. Super! You will save time, distress, and money.

But you still need a proofreader. Hopefully one who will challenge every word and phrase, then ask at the end of every sentence and paragraph, "How could that be better or more clearly said?" A saint who will go beyond spelling and punctuation to delete repetition (particularly redundant repetition), useless jargon, pointless humor, and anything else that decreases the reader's perception of you as an expert worthy of further consultation about matters that count.

If you use a ghost or rewriter, do you need a proofreader? It depends upon whether the first person also proofreads — and how well. Ask them to proof, if they do that. Then ask a friend who is a critical reader whether they think the piece still needs proofing. If in doubt, get it proofed!

What do you pay proofreaders? About $25 an hour, but the range may run from $12-40. Have them write the changes above or by the text so you can see each item before you alter the draft. Sometimes proofreaders simply don't understand what you must convey so their proposed modifications don't work for your readership. Often they delete needed humor — or don't know why you used a certain "in" word that is crucial to show your readers that you are one of them. Go over every change first, then ask how the points of contention can be rewritten to meet the proofer's objection and your need.

Where do you find these angels of prose? Ask other writers in your field. Check the *Literary Market Place* (see editorial assistance) and the ads in *Writer's Digest Magazine* and *The Writer* in your library. Newspaper and advertising folk often moonlight here. I've had excellent success with librarians. Try faculty in the communications and English departments of your local college. Check your local phone book under "writing." Ask around. Also verify the current going rate for the various services in the *Writer's Market* of that year, again at the library.

A final, necessary thought. What happens later when you are asked to write something, to replicate that "surefooted, fast prose" that you bought from somebody else? Two and a half answers. One, if you are no further along with written expression than you were the day you found the ghost or rewriter, find that same person again — or another as gifted. Two, if you've mastered the skill, what's the problem? Do it, then get it proofed. But if you're half way in between, better now that you've seen how it's done but still a bit heavy-footed and stolid, write first, then get a rewriter to touch it up. In short, do what must be done to bring solid information well written to a hungry market. Accept no compromise on either the information or the writing.

SPEAKING

If you can't speak at all, you must limit the ways you directly share your expertise to written formats. Or you can script what you want to say on tape or disc and have others say it for you. You could even give talks, speeches, or seminars if you and your audience sign; that is, if your target market is the hearing or speaking impaired.

But most newcomers can speak well enough, or could if it weren't for that audience they had to face! So they need to work on other things to rise to the level of proficiency required to earn top dollars this way.

The oral means discussed in this book can be divided into two categories: indirect and direct. Indirect means that you speak, it is recorded, and listeners turn you on at their convenience. Those means include audio and video tapes and other forms of discs. Direct means that you speak directly to the listener, as you do at talks, speeches, seminars, and consulting.

Let's discuss them in that order.

For indirect speaking several things are required: a clear speaking script, integrated visual scripting and action for a video tape, craftsmanship to capture the voice (and movement), a voice that will convey the message well (with all the needed inflections and modulations), and a solid, preferably flawless, presentation.

You can hire the craftspeople to properly capture your voice and movement, as we discussed in earlier chapters. For a video they will also assist in the visual scripting and action.

Which leaves the script and the speaking.

You use the same techniques to produce a well written script that you use to write an article or a book, except you hire a ghost or rewriter experienced in oral presentation or script writing. You bring the ideas, the things you want to say, the words that must be used, the facts and quotes and anecdotes and anything else that must be shared, and they put it into lively, comprehensible, expertise-enhancing prose.

You lay the groundwork, they write the script, and then you work on it together until it sounds like you, but clearer, quicker, at full force.

If you speak like a burly longshoreman with a no-nonsense vocabulary, your audience is burly longshoremen using the same vernacular, and your script makes you sound like the Queen's poet-laureate, they won't hear you over their laughter. That's why you iron out the differences with your scriptwriting helper, so that you sound like you. Otherwise it's no help at all, you won't be believed, and you're better off keeping your mouth shut, limiting yourself to writing, or simply fading back into the other 99%.

Then there's the voice. As we said earlier, voice coaches can work wonders. But they work best against a taped example, so you take the final script, tape it as you want it to sound (or as close as you can come), and let them guide you from there. Read the script several times first. Learn to pronounce each word properly. Underline the words and phrases that must be stressed. Then practice the script aloud a couple of times before you turn on your home recorder. Rest for a while, then tape — nonstop the first time, then stopping as needed thereafter. Produce a good tape, share it with the coach, and all that remains is the final taping session and recorded posterity!

Direct speaking is harder because you perform unaided, you alone in front of them. You can pass out — quickly is kinder for all concerned. You can mispronounce every word, put every punchline before its setup, see your audience slide into a motionless trance, watch it rise en masse and stomp out, have a heckler shout invectives from your first word to your last, be hit by hurled vegetation, be physically dragged from the microphone....

Those are the things you usually dream about the night preceding your first professional speech. So your goal is to prepare so completely, know your material so well, and practice so often and intensely that there is no way that any of those demons could possibly obstruct your stellar presentation.

In short, you hire writing and coaching help as needed. And you prepare and practice fully. But you might also do some other speaking first if you simply aren't a natural, gifted orator.

To reiterate a bit, Toastmasters is an excellent place to learn the basics, present to peers, and get constructive criticism on the spot. It's unimportant at this level that you won't be speaking about your niche specialty. In fact, it's better. Not only can you focus more on learning speaking skills when you address other topics, your niche audience won't hear you at your crack-voiced, knee-knocking worst.

A good second step is talking to local and regional nonpaying organizations, such as the service clubs, lodges, churches, and sports organizations. Devise a talk that lasts from 12 to 20 minutes about a topic they want to know, prepare an attractive one-page information flyer about the talk and you, send it to the program chairs, and follow up with a telephone call. Remember to put some humor in your talk: they're not paying you nothing to be bored!

There's another approach. Find a cause and be its spokesperson for a year. Tell the clubs and organizations why they should support the United Way, a hospice, the Scouts, or perhaps some local program for wildlife preservation. It's an easy booking, listeners will think well of you for giving your time and skill to further that cause, and you are developing your own speaking proficiency in the doing.

Then there's the kamikaze technique. Create an excellent script, using the help needed; practice until your delivery is at par with other speaking professionals, again with as much coaching as you need, then jump in. Get booked or create a speaking opportunity and speak. Count on the niche audience's strategic interest in your topic, plus your preparedness, to pull you through. Then do it again, and again, until you are in fact the best speaker on that topic that your nichefolk could hear, and just about the best on any topic you might develop.

Chapter 16

Profiting from Others'
Niche Marketing

You really can be devoid of expressive skills and turn our kind of niche marketing into your own kind of profits. Just find a writer or speaker who has the ideas and the skills! Sounds parasitic but it can be a triple victory: for them, for the people who need the information, and, of course, for old number one — you!

Here are some ways that you can profit from others' niche marketing:

(1) Help put them into niche marketing. America abounds with smart, talented people. Yet many, gifted in one way, are almost useless (or think themselves so) in other ways. Many are bristling with concepts, processes, and ideas but can't sit still long enough to put them on paper. Still others are great at putting things on paper, love to sit, but couldn't find a new concept if they were looking through it.

So what you can do is define your strengths, list your weaknesses, and find an equal who is strong where you are weak. How many great things never reach reality because the thinker/planner isn't a maker/seller?

It's clear, then. Two (or more) instead of one defining a niche, meeting a critical need, and spreading out to meet that need better, then meeting more, related needs by the same and other means. You are the catalyst and accomplice who helps take the basic information and put it into niche circulation. But be very clear (best on paper) who does what, who gets what, and what happens if the merging of talents and personalities goes sour.

(2) If a person is well established in a niche through either writing or speaking but shows no evidence (or perhaps skill) of developing further, why not suggest some sort of combined approach to sharing needed information by complementary means with the buying field that you share in common?

For example, this person may publish regularly in the niche trade magazines, have one or many books out, and even be the author of a key report — but be utterly incapable of, or simply not interested in, delivering speeches or offering seminars. Which is what you do well, are known for in the niche orb, and want to continue to do.

Why not pool talents, dually dominate your interest field, complement each other by cross-selling the other's products, and over time probably fuse talents to take your information as far and by as many means as work, each of you contributing the skills you do best? But, again, first define roles and expectations clearly.

(3) Sometimes a niche field is dotted with lesser players but no dominant figure. That could be you, at least financially. If one person creates tapes, another published a book, another offers seminars, and a fourth gives speeches, an opening exists for you to bring all of this together and become the niche impresario.

Why not put all of their products and services into a classy catalog, broker or sell them, create a master mailing list of potential customers in the niche field in the process, and use that as the core of drawing all of the idea disseminators into your organization or sphere of influence? Why not start a newsletter with each of the lesser stars as participants? Why not a conference or convention where they perform and you sell, including your newsletter subscriptions?

You can become the publisher in the field, of books, reports, and tapes. You can develop new, lesser stars (by your perception): as they grow and create new products, your empire of intermediacy will also grow.

Sound a bit overly avaricious or vulturistic? Many talented people can only flourish when somebody else removes the business burden and deals honestly and supportively with them. Others may be less eager to share the wealth, but you provide the best and most profitable venue for their success, short of replicating what you have created, so they will cooperate. And a few won't. But there are other, lesser stars who can do basically what they do, and they will cooperate.

The real skill here, it seems to me, is to infuse the entire field with a sense of cooperativeness, giving each due credit for their excellence in their respective expertise. And you quietly accept the credit for your expertise in making good information readily available in quality form at reasonable prices to all in the niche market. To succeed here you would need some starting capital, a clear vision of where you fit into the grander scheme, diplomacy, plenty of promotion, and tenacity.

(4) Is somebody already there? If there is a dominant figure doing roughly what I just described, he or she is likely mortal. Mortals grow weary, broke, sick, old, or dead. Sorry to mention that. But at any of those points, except the last, they may be giddy with delight should you offer to buy them out. Then you infuse new blood into the structure, dust off your diplomacy, and get to building a selling core for the constellation of other stars eager to shine through your support and encouragement.

(5) Let's look at profiting from a different angle. In this book I have focused on 13 means of idea dissemination to niche markets. Each of those means is like sand in an hourglass: at some point the information merchant using it must rely upon somebody else for the information to be offered in its final form.

Books, for example, usually need graphics and art specialists for covers and illustrations, printers, proofreaders, barcode film manufacturers, fulfillment folk to respond to orders, distributors....

Why couldn't you specialize in that peculiar field for niche marketed products in general? For example, why couldn't you be the hourglass gatekeeper for book design for tightly-targeted, limited distribution books? The niche would be far less important than your broader understanding of how niche marketed books sell, what designs work, how the costs can be kept minimal, how a basic design could be expanded into a theme for a series of books, how that cover design could be integrated into all of one's products and graphic representations (like a logo), how the design could be easily duplicated in various sizes for later incorporation while the cover is being completed, and so on....

I recently began a service that fits plunk into this category — before I even knew there was a category! It is a clear example of how others' expertise can play a critical role in the niche arena.

Called "The Pathfinder," I read, evaluate, and constructively advise others about their books-in-development at one of two key points: (1) when it's in its final organizational and design form but before the text is written, and (2) when the final draft is complete but before it's begun production. The purpose is to help the writer define (or refine) the vision, see how the book is achieving that, discuss any alterations that will make the book sell better, and help infuse necessary marketing and design modifications into the text from the outset.

I use this example only to show how in all of the means there are critical points where knowledgeable outside help can guide the information bearers into the most productive, best, easiest, least expensive paths.

If you are eager to take part in the coming niche marketing avalanche but your expertise is broader, see if it can't be refined to help lead the product producers or service-givers in ways similar to those suggested.

A final way too. The grander field of niche marketing has yet to be plowed. Tillers are needed. People to help the newcomers properly plant and reap. This book barely scratches the surface of a side moor: niche marketing by writing and speaking. More books and guides are necessary, to clarify what is hinted at here, to instruct those with information that cries to be heard, to help them make it widely, instantly, and rewardingly available to others who will, in turn, use it to improve the world.

There are other ways too that clever entrepreneurs will ferret out to profit from others' niche marketing.

In another sense, we all directly profit from niche marketers, though it may not be evident in our daily income. Information is the oil of today's society. Niche marketers are targeting and imparting specific information in a way thought impossible just a decade or two back. From knowledge and ideas come change, and from change the prospect of a better life. But that's enough musing.

Chapter 17

Keeping It All Together for a Lifetime Yield

What makes it possible for you to focus on a niche market and sell to it time and again is the quality of the advice or information you give it, your accessibility to that market, how often you go to it, and the rapport you create and maintain between yourself and your buyers.

That all starts with what you're selling. Dumb stuff, things they would never in their lives care to know about, something they learned years ago, or flat-out unreliable information — not a solid foundation on that sea of sand called buyer loyalty.

Let me assume that what I have said in the preceding 16 chapters has helped you define what niche market buyers want and are likely to purchase. And further assume that you will start, or quickly get to, something vital or central to their needs, so that by the time you are thinking of converting your early sales, or even your first-time market contact, into a high-paying, lifelong source of income you already have your niche market fully aware of who you are, why it should pay attention to what you sell, and salivating at the chance to buy the next product you offer.

If the quality is there, accessibility is crucial for long-range success. That means you not only have direct access to the niche market, it is the right market, you are mailing to enough of it, and you are sending to the right addresses.

Most niche marketers begin by renting the best mailing lists they can find, or afford, when circulating their first flyer. The names of those who respond then become the core of their own mailing list. They will probably continue to rent other lists for a while, culling the repetitions between their list and the rented one(s). (If both lists are computerized you can do this through the merge-purge process. If they are pressure-sensitive labels, you can simply pluck out the duplications before labeling them or after, by putting them into global zip code piles and pasting other labels over the duplicates.)

When you start creating your own mailing list it is important that you determine precisely what you want to know. Central to any list is the person's name, the company name (if important), the street address (with apartment or suite) or box number, city, state, and ZIP.

Beyond that some lists are broken down by the products bought (you can code, say, by book, giving each a different letter, or by the means, with one letter for books bought, another for seminar registration, another for newsletter subscription), by correspondence or information solicitation only, by services purchased, by the dollar amount of the order (again, a letter for each dollar range), or by any other category that will make sense later when you want to target a specific sub-niche for tight mailing. (If you keep your list current you will be able to tell the approximate date of the last contact by the date of computer entry.)

Once you know what you need to record, create paperwork that will solicit that information. For example, develop a phone-answering information sheet to complete so every caller gets into the mailing list as fully as you wish (sometimes irksome, uncooperative people give you what they think you need to know!) The same with order forms on your flyers. Include what you want to know — and leave the lines open enough so your customers can fit it in!

Then impress upon the person entering the data in your computer mailing list to take care that the facts are accurate and the additional information is fully coded. (Keep a current *National ZIP Code and Post Office Directory* at hand to accurately enter the codes when they are illegible, partial, or imaginary.)

There is a way to supplement your list quickly. If your niche buyers belong to a trade or professional association, or similar group, join it and get a membership list. Enter this list in your computer and mail to it several times. When a buyer from it orders or responds, delete them from the membership list as you put them on your own list. After a certain point mailing to the few who have repeatedly failed to respond will prove unproductive and you can abandon that membership list. Also, keep the master list the group sends you from year to year, compare this year's with last, and create a new, small list of additional names.

Be diligent about finding new names and lists for your niche market. In Chapter 5 we discuss "Qualifying and Nichifying your Market," and direct you to the *Standard Rate and Data Services Mailing Lists* and the *Encyclopedia of Associations* for starters, and suggest that you see what else your niche buyers are sent, like magazines, newsletters, card decks, flyers, seminar registration solicitations, ads, and more. Those don't arrive by chance: ask the senders where they got their mailing list. If it's their own, see if you can rent it — after checking its origin, how often it's cleaned, the cost, any restrictions on its use, and so on.

Crucial to your long-term success in dealing repeatedly with the same niche group is the accuracy and fullness of your own mailing list, so work hard to make it the very best possible. Actively seek new names. When you mail to your own list by bulk rate, include "Address Correction Requested" below your return address on every item so all those not delivered will be returned to you with the reason why, and usually the new forwarding address. Also check the post office to see about their address updating system. It's a bit serpentine to use but accurate and inexpensive.

A final thought: should you rent out your list once it's sizable, accurate, and clean? There are two schools of thought: one, why give away for a nickel or so a name what it cost three to four times as much to get, keep, clean, and service? And why help the competition?

On the other hand, it's an expensive tool to maintain alone. Why not earn as much, or much more, from the list by renting it out regularly? You have a control so it doesn't directly compete with you: require approval of the items to be sent to it, then seed your list with entries who will send you everything they receive in the mail to their coded name (usually you give them the wrong first name). If you feel the item is too close to your line, reject it. And if they mail out something other than what you approved or they use the list more than once, get on them. Perhaps take them to court. Certainly don't rent to them again.

The key point is accessibility. At least you need reliable mailing lists to get to your target market. Soon enough, you will need your own list.

A final thought concerning accessibility. If you can get to your targeted market, your niche buyers, always keep open the possibility that there are more potential eager buyers that you are not approaching or reaching.

Note any person, group, type, vocation, hobbyist, and wild-catter who shares the same basic need you meet. Start with your chosen niche market, then move out. Do that by age, by geographic spread, by related or shared similarities, by relative position (for example, from a middle-manager to top manager and boss or lower-middle to new employee), from one sex to the other, and so on.

If the same product or service is sold to the new unit(s) the same way, simply expand your list and your marketing. But if it requires modifications, think that completely through before blithely tinkering at the lower level. How does that seemingly modest change to a new market affect your greater positioning in your primary field? Don't end up like my medical friend whose business cards read "Dr. ____, brain surgeon and venetian blind repairman"!

How often you mail to your list is another factor. Office supply wholesalers send me catalogs, updates, new product releases, and "special sale" material, it seems, hourly. I assume that is sufficiently profitable and about the right time spread in their highly competitive field.

On the other hand, book publishers from whom I buy mail twice a year. We send seminar information sheets to the California segment of our list at least once, usually twice a year, as part of our catalog. That works well. More and the sales return doesn't justify the additional labor and postage — unless we have a "hot" product our niche market needs instantly, like this book!

Others wait until they have a product, market it aggressively, and include an add-on segment selling whatever else they offer that niche market.

There are two ways to see what is the best mailing balance for you: practice and seeing what the competition (or those selling similar items) does, assuming the competition is solvent and has been actively marketing long enough to have created a profitable working pattern.

If you're in doubt about going out the second or third time after a product has been launched, do a test mailing: 100, 500, 1000. Select a specific segment of your list (usually by ZIP code or alphabetically) or an "nth" selection — every twelfth name or the name every three-quarters of an inch. You should easily sell enough to cover the cost of the test. If you don't, aren't you happy you ran a small test?

Another point is how often and what you sell to your niche market. If you are new, you have just mailed your first flyer featuring your ground-breaking product, and it is a huge success — say 15% of your market buys it, — reslant that flyer and go out again. But the wisdom of mailing a flyer featuring that product only a third time or more must be questioned.

Consider highlighting a new product by you in that third mailing — giving it top billing, with the original product still prominently featured — plus some additional, key items by others, to create a mini-catalog. Also note high in prominence in that mailing something like: "A new catalog of indispensable (products, services, ...) for _____ (niche buyers) on page __!"

Make sure those products *are* indispensable. You will be judged by everything you sell so only add the best items. Read, see, hear — review everything compatible and supportive of your position and product(s). Pick only those that substantially enhance your reputation. Don't hesitate to feature products from the other leaders in your field. In fact, talk with them, tell them why you like their product(s), of your coming catalog, of your interest in adding those items to it, then try to get a better volume discount for buying in lot, nonrefundable. (Should their books be returned to you for refund — usually because they were damaged in the mail — simply sell them at your seminars or B.O.R. table at what they cost you: the price and shipping minus discount. That might happen to an item or two a year.) We usually buy from others whom we feature in our catalog at 50% off — and sell our products to them at the same discount.

Later on you might have two kinds of product listings. For example, we now have a modest, annually updated in-house catalog that features our products only. That is sent with every order filled — or when requested. (In the beginning, though, we had so few items we included all products, ours and others', in one catalog.)

With our catalog we also send one (or more) of four "Where to find additional information about..." single, full-paged sheets, each listing specific books, tapes, and reports about (1) writing articles and books, (2) writing travel articles that sell, (3) speaking and empire-building, and (4) self-publishing. Those include our products and the best of others', each with several lines of explanation. With them goes a full-page order form that includes every item we currently sell.

How do we decide who gets which of the four, plus the catalog and order form? By what they order from us. If they buy my *Travel Writer's Guide* or anything specifically travel-related, for example, they get (2) above. On it they read about some additional key items by Rohn Engh and Ann Burgess (plus the current *Writer's Market*) that we are happy to offer. If they want that book plus my *Self-Publishing to Tightly-Targeted Markets*, they get (2) plus (4), which tells of other top items they should know about by Poynter, Kremer, Zoerner, Barker, and both Bunnin and Beren.

Other information disseminators we know have one or many in-house, their-products-only catalogs or flyers — plus another that features valuable, supplementary products they sell.

Why bother with others' products? To meet your niche market's needs, to keep their focus primarily on you and your key offerings (they needn't leave your store, or catalog, to also buy other things), to reinforce your position as being at least one of the leaders in your field, to benefit indirectly from the association with the other leaders (by being, at least on paper, a product equal), to help offset the cost of promotion and marketing through the additional income selling others' products brings, and to profit from their sales.

Would I sell others' products at the outset? Probably not. First I'd sell my own, vital product that my niche market desperately needs. And probably create a second product, then spread out by bringing in the best of the rest — yet always keeping them in the background, as supportive, position- and profit-enhancing add-ons, like french fries at MacDonalds.

The rapport you create and maintain with your niche buyers is critical in determining your long-range success in the field — plus how often those in it will tolerate your returning to sell them products.

First you must get their attention. That is best done by excelling in some or every way. Offer a product they very much need. Then more topflight products. All the while a growing recognition of you as a leader, a key player, in the field.

When your singular area of excellence comes to mind or is mentioned, so is your name. Conversely, when your name comes up, so does the focal point of your expertise.

Then you must continue to maintain your presence, lest that hard-earned acceptance and recognition irreparably slip.

You don't earn others' esteem by simply flaunting, bullying, or by just outproducing the rest. You get there by having something worth esteeming, then selling it honestly, humbly, and with utmost concern for those buying it. The usual virtues are required: clarity, courtesy, humility, and love.

"Surely God would not have created such a being as man ... to exist for only one day! No, no, man was made for immortality."

Abraham Lincoln (1804-1865)

"I don't want to achieve immortality through my work, I want to achieve it through not dying."

Woody Allen

Chapter 18

Niche Marketing for More Than Money

Throughout this book I've spoken of financial wealth and how niche marketing can lead you to it. Which is true.

But there are many other, valuable reasons for sharing information that have little to do with money, and they too must be addressed.

One is close to my heart, having spent many formative years in academia. Information is gathered, analyzed, tested, compared, and then shared so that people can collectively learn. From that learning we can improve our lives and our environment, avoid mistakes made from ignorance, and expand our capacity to learn even more, faster, and with greater certainty.

That is the world of the biochemist toiling repetitively on a singular experiment, its object minute but its significance inordinately large. The results are shared in an article in an obscure journal read and comprehended by at most 500 like souls worldwide. No lifetime foothold on wealth, little notoriety beyond the 500, the thinnest slice of immortality, yet a huge leap forward in man's grasp of nature's hold.

It's the same quiet, limited expansion of new ideas, proven facts, and original concepts that has guided us from the perpetuation of history through folk songs and passed tales to the multifaceted information explosion through CD-ROM and CD-I.

It's the restrained and unobtrusive sharing of the historian, research psychologist, archaeologist, visual arts instructor, swimming trainer, and volcanologist. All niche sharing and niche marketing in their own sedate and usually profitless — but cumulatively momentous — ways.

Another reason to share valuable information, to niche market without a clear vision of profit, is to pay back something to a society, people, or world for what you have received. To pay off the debt of being able to live well at the expense of many. To pay back the other toilers who have historically moved life to where it is and where you are, and to recompense those who have made your life and good fortune possible.

A third reason is to help create a better world for your children and their children. As Handel composed *The Messiah*, somebody grew the cotton in the clothes you wear, Dr. Salk developed the polio vaccine, and your teachers learned the importance of infusing students like you with self-esteem — of a million examples that make your world better than life was millennia back — you too move the world to a higher plain by sharing specific information to be spread into the future.

And anyway, you're only around once. This is it. You must validate your existence. You can be remembered as the meanest, cruelest, most useless hunk of humanity ever to insult the flesh. Which will give you a wee but vile nick of immortality.

Or you can be remembered as a giving, sharing, positive person who made a difference. Any special information shared is the ticket to the latter club.

It may be earthshaking: the cure to AIDs or cancer, the explanation of black holes, a formula for maintaining a steady-balance state with nature, a new insight that will draw fighting philosophies and utter enemies to a harmonious world camp.

Or it may be smaller but perhaps no less significant: the loving creation of a family, a suggestion to improve productivity at work, writing a novel or play that lets us see ourselves more fully or in a different light, an open hand or way to help another through a period of deprivation or despair...

By expansion, those are forms of niche marketing. Niching, from a specific few to many, marketing by sharing but here without the purpose of monetary gain.

Alas, whether recompense is the purpose or even a motivating factor, information has value. The spread of that information, the sharing of its worth, and a reward for the sharer — monetary or otherwise — have been the purpose of this book.

There are ways that niche marketing can indeed make you indispensable, slightly immortal, and even lifelong rich. We have explained how that can be done. But by whatever path you pursue it, we are all enriched by niche marketing and we are grateful for your having done it and shared.

BIBLIOGRAPHY
and
RECOMMENDED READING

Anderson, Jim. *Speaking to Groups: Eyeball to Eyeball.* Wyndmoor Press, Vienna, VA. 1989.

Barker, Malcolm. *Book Design and Production.* Londonborn Pubs., San Francisco, CA. 1990 (*)

Beach, Mark. *Editing Your Newsletter*, second ed. Coast to Coast Books, Portland, OR. 1982.

Bedrosian, Margaret. *Speak Like a Pro.* John Wiley & Sons, New York, NY. 1987.

Bermont, Hubert. *How to Become a Successful Consultant in Your Own Field*, third rev. ed. Prima Publishing, Rocklin, CA. 1991.

Buck, Tony. "A Publisher's Intro. to CD-I." Report by Tony Buck, Merion Station, PA. 1992.

Bunnin, Brad, and Peter Beren. *The Writer's Legal Companion.* Addison-Wesley Pub. Co., Reading, MA. 1988. (*)

Burgett, Gordon. *Writer's Guide to Query Letters and Cover Letters.* Prima Publishing, Rocklin, CA. 1992 (*)

_____. *How to Sell More Than 75% of Your Freelance Writing.* Prima Publishing, Rocklin, CA. 1990 (*)

_____. *Self-Publishing to Tightly-Targeted Markets.* Communication Unlimited, Santa Maria, CA. 1989 (*)

_____. *Empire-Building by Writing and Speaking.* Communication Unlimited, Santa Maria, CA. 1987 (*)

_____. "How to Set Up and Market Your Own Seminar," 3-hour audiotape series. Communication Unlimited, Santa Maria, CA. 1990 (*)

_____. "Producing and Selling Your Own Audiocassettes," 1-hour audiotape. Communication Unlimited, Santa Maria, CA. 1991 (*)

_____. "Speakers: How to Penetrate Your Market and Earn a Bundle of Money With Your First Book," 45-minute audiotape. Communication Unlimited, Santa Maria, CA. 1990

_____. "How to Sell Your Book to General and Niche Markets," 3-hour audiotape series. Communication Unlimited, Santa Maria, CA . 1993 (*)

Burgett, Gordon, and Dr. Cyril Zoerner, Jr. "Case Study: Textbook for a Tightly-Targeted Market," report. Communication Unlimited, Santa Maria, CA. 1991 (*)

Burgett, Gordon, and Mike Frank. *Speaking for Money*. Communication Unlimited, Santa Maria, CA. 1985 (*)

Engh, Rohn. *How to Sell and Re-Sell Your Photos*, third ed.. Writer's Digest Books, Cincinnati, OH. 1991 (*)

Fettig, Art. *How to Hold an Audience in the Hollow of Your Hand*, second ed. Growth Unlimited, Battle Creek, MI. 1988.

Floyd, Elaine. *Marketing With Newsletters*. EF Communications, St. Louis, MO. 1991.

Holtz, Herman. *The Consultant's Guide to Newsletter Profits*. Dow Jones-Irwin, Homewood, IL. 1987.

Hudson, Howard Penn. *Publishing Newsletters*, rev. ed. Charles Scribner's Sons, New York, NY. 1988.

Kremer, John. *1001 Ways to Market Your Books*, third ed. Ad-Lib Pubs., Fairfield, IA. 1990 (*)

Oxford Directory of Newsletters. Oxford Communications, New York, NY. Current edition.

Poynter, Dan. *The Self-Publishing Manual*, sixth ed. Para Publishing, Santa Barbara, CA. 1991 (*)

Poynter, Dan, and Charles Kent. *Publishing Contracts: Sample Agreements for Book Publishers on Disk*. Para Publishing, Santa Barbara, CA. 1987.

Schumacher, Michael. *The Writer's Complete Guide to Conducting Interviews*. Writer's Digest Books, Cincinnati. 1993 (*)

Stone, Bob. *Successful Direct Selling*. NTC Pub. Group, Lincolnwood, IL. 1985

Standard Directory of Newsletters. Oxbridge Pub., New York, NY. Current edition.

Walters, Dottie and Lillet. *Speak and Grow Rich*. Prentice-Hall, Englewood Cliffs, NJ. 1989 (*)

Wheeler, Eugene, and Rennie Mau. Let Your Ideas Speak Out: A Guide to Preparing and Marketing Spoken Words on Audiotape and CDs. Pathfinder Pub., Ventura, CA. 1991.

Writer's Market. Writer's Digest Books, Cincinnati. Annual. (*)

(*) The newest edition of this book is available through Communication Unlimited. See the order form on the last page for information.

INDEX